There Are
NO OLD PEOPLE
in HEAVEN

You're Not Getting Old, You're Getting Ready

STEVE LYON

ARIEL WRITING

To Jesus Christ
My God, King, Savior, and Friend
After all You've done for me,
How can I not dedicate the first of
our labor together to You?

ACKNOWLEDGMENTS

I t's standard fare for authors to pause here and thank those who've helped them escort an idea God has hidden in the tunnel-dark caverns of their gray matter to the incandescence of a book. I assure you, none has ever offered it with more sincerity than me.

To my faithful friend of forty-five years, Dr. John Trent; Dr. Gary Brinkley; and friends Linda Boss, Nita Sheffield, Faith McCoppin, and Rick Swetman: a multitude of thanks for your insights and suggestions in the early stages of the manuscript and cover design. Along those lines, a special shout out to another great friend of forty-plus years, Dr. Fred Chay, whose sharp theological eye helped refine and shape key elements of His truth. And to Larry Libby, whose kindness in honest feedback proved a true blessing and that time and distance don't diminish the truth old friends really are the best friends. To all of you, your encouragement and support means more than you know. This book is a better representation of our Lord and His Truth because of you. Thank you.

To Steve Kuhn, whose professional expertise, creativity, and care brought life to the interior and cover design. I knew you would do a great job! To Jane Friedmann and Dale L. Roberts who, though we've never met, provided invaluable assistance on self-publishing through their web presence. I couldn't have done it without you guys.

Finally, special thanks to my wife, Dawn, who believed in me and trusted our Lord enough to allow me the freedom to write while she worked to provide for our needs—and who applied her formidable eye for detail to editing the manuscript. Both are examples of how the Lord uses her remarkable blend of goodness, giftedness, and mature faith to bless me beyond anything I deserve. Every day, she proves, "He who finds a wife finds a good thing and obtains favor from the Lord" (Proverbs 18:22). Dawn, I love you with all my heart and am more thankful for our life together than you know. Thanks for enabling me to add to the work of His kingdom in a way I pray will outlive our time on earth. I am always,

Together With You for Him,
Steve Lyon
Cedar Park, Texas
November 2021

CONTENTS

The righteous thrive like a palm tree
And grow like a cedar tree in Lebanon.
Planted in the house of the Lord,
They thrive in the courts of our God.
They still bear fruit in old age,
Healthy and green, to declare:
The Lord is just;
He is my rock,
And there is no unrighteousness in Him

PSALM 92:12-15, HCSB

⟨⟩

Your dead will live
Their bodies will rise,
Awake and sing, you who dwell in the dust!
For you will be covered with the morning dew,
And the earth will bring out the departed spirits

ISAIAH 26:19, HCSB

Chapter 1

I GUESS HE MISSED THE MEMO

I was having a hard time getting my arms around the question. It was Christmas Day and the family was together, along with a friend of the family I'd never met, a mortgage broker in his thirties who would have\ been by himself otherwise. Naturally, we were glad he could join us.

Most who know me will tell you I can start a conversation with just about anyone, so within a few minutes my new friend and I were engaged and enjoying the interaction. We talked sports and I asked about his family. He grew up in another part of the state and his siblings and step-siblings were spread across the country. I was curious about his path to mortgage banking. He described how he started in financial services, found it less than fulfilling, and decided helping people buy homes was a more gratifying way to make a living. I affirmed that's a good thing and commended him for doing so.

That's when he asked the question.

The one I should have anticipated but in no way expected.

"So," he said with all the innocence of an eight-year-old asking Uncle Steve if he wanted to go outside and play catch.

"Are you retired?"

"I'm sorry." I thought. "Am I what? What did he just ask me?" I scrambled to winch my chin up from my knees, hoping he didn't notice the stunned look on my face.

Self-talk quickly ensued. "Now wait just a minute, Mr. Thirty-Something-Broker Man. People tell me I look young for my age and you… you want to know if I'm ruh… ruh… uh, ruh… (Sorry. It's still hard to get the words out). You want to know if I, ummm… no longer work?"

It wasn't the question, per se. He could have been asking out of the sincere pulse of envy I used to feel when *I* was a thirty-something, looking over the work-infested, hassle-laden decades ahead, wishing all of it was behind me and I could stick my toes in the warm sands of retirement.

It's what the question implied, that based on the semi-alien form staring at him—the mutinous physique, the hair gone AWOL, the din of my baby blues, the timbre of my voice—it was perfectly realistic and not-at-all offensive to assume I must have reached the point where my abilities and worth had slouched enough that I needed to slink out the door of the working world before I was *shown* the door.

"Does this grasshopper think I've lost my 'A' game," I thought, "that I spend my days complaining about dry skin and bunions, the first question I ask when the server hands me the menu is, 'Where is the men's room?' and most Sunday afternoons find me sleepy-slumping in an easy chair watching golf? Is *that* what he thinks?"

Thankfully, as the spear of his curiosity penetrated the veneer of my youth, an encouraging thought came to mind, one from the benevolent hand of the Almighty, no doubt. "This poor guy *obviously* doesn't understand I'm from the blessed generation; the first in history endowed by our Creator with the unalienable right to do what we've always done with as much physical prowess and mental dexterity as when we were twenty-five. Sure, there's a touch of gray here and there and I can't eat what I used to. Those things aside, it should be obvious my pack and I just rolled off the showroom floor. I guess he missed the memo."

∼∼∼

I sure wish that memo was real.

Don't you?

Truth be told, in the split second it took for his question to travel from my ear to my brain, shuffle past all the rationalizations, and land in my heart, I went from feeling really *with* it to knowing I was really *without* it.

Youth is not my birthright. The ability to do as I've always done and be as I always imagined is a mirage. I know you know what I'm talking about. Lung capacity diminishes. Hearts have a harder time beating and beat more often just to keep up. Veins and arteries clog and harden. Muscles, once saturated with strength, speed, and agility, can't lift as much, react as fast, or run as far. They require more rest after less effort. A throw sure feels good on a chilly June evening.

Then there's the mental side of the ledger. Neurons short circuit. Brains become less elastic and nimble. We take in just as much and remember less. Confusion comes calling more often. The effort to stay with it and keep up hardly seems worth it. We care less about how we look. Plaid and stripes work. Ditto for knee-high dress socks and shorts—or bra straps playing hide-and-seek with tank tops. So what if the waistband on our underwear is frayed and the elastic ain't what it used to be? It stays up—most of the time. I mean hey, a penny saved, right? We're on a fixed income these days. Score one for being frugal.

You and I know better. Growing old is the pits. It's embarrassing. It makes us feel bad. It kills us to think we may be a burden to our kids. We realize that just as happened with our parents, the day may come when our offspring ask us to hand over the car keys. Or have to help with our diaper. Or tell us it's time to sell the house.

Sure, as believers in Jesus Christ we know He promises the one who dies will live again (John 11:25). But that's then. It's hard to think about "then" when "now" means decay, grief, and too many goodbyes. We've seen how much all that hurts. We know often, the sting never completely goes away.

And it doesn't just happen to other people. It's happening to *me*—and you. We're reminded every day our youth and energy is like soap; the more we've used, the less we have. And death, well … the closer it gets, the faster it comes. As English poet and clergyman John Donne famously said centuries ago: "Ask not for whom the bell tolls. It tolls for thee."

Old age and death stalk us. Ferociously.

Sure, we can run. We can feign, dodge, and duck all we want. But we cannot hide.

I should tell you about something another friend of the family said. His name was Curtis Lashley and unlike the mortgage broker, I'd known him for decades. Like the broker, he was in his thirties when I met him. I was in second or third grade. He was our family doctor, possessed of a warm, gentle-yet-confident personality and a penchant for underplayed yet hysterical practical jokes.

Case in point: His father-in-law, Joe Garrison, was a true-blue, dyed-in-the-wool Presbyterian minister. One day, Joe erroneously called Curtis thinking he'd contacted a national store chain to check on a pending delivery. Curtis immediately realized his mistake and masqueraded as a friendly yet bumbling service person who couldn't for the life of him figure out what happened to the order.

Knowing the good reverend's professional decorum and moral code wouldn't allow him to fully express his frustration, he poured it on. The more Curtis feigned confusion, the more Joe chafed with mounting strains of "Good … *GRIEF!!!*—delighting Curtis like a kid brother whose sister just discovered he put a frog in her dresser. It was only when Curtis thought Joe was a few seconds from a convulsion of depraved speech that might ruin his ministry that he clued him in. Hilarious.

That kind of quick, playful wit is one of the things that made Curtis and his wife, Terry, good friends with my parents. They were four peas in a pod. When it was time for the Lyons to expand their square footage to accommodate three active children, the Lashley's sold my Mom and Dad the property next door so they could build a home and we could be neighbors.

A few years later, God called my dad to a job on the other side of the country. The routine, neighborly interaction quelled—but thankfully, the affection did not. Over the decades, as both sets of children grew and both sets of parents grew old, the connection continued through calls, letters, and visits when God brought them about.

One day, we learned Curtis had suffered a stroke. His recovery was marked with the lingering shadows of paralysis and some difficulty speaking. Thankfully, he made something of a comeback. Then word came he was sick again—and this time it looked like the end.

As death approached, the family took turns at his bedside. In one of those moments, he told them he and Joe (who'd preceded him to heaven by a good bit) had been talking and Joe told him, "Curtis, it's about time for you to come up here." In another, his youngest daughter, Claire, noticed he was looking intently at the ceiling, his concentration never wavering.

Finally, she asked, "What are you looking at, Dad?"

"I'm looking into heaven," he replied. "And it's just so beautiful I can't take my eyes off it." Not too long after, the good doctor and good friend, the man who'd blessed our family with healing and humor, handed his stethoscope to His Lord and went home.

<hr/>

Do you believe that story?

I do. Without doubt or hesitation. I knew the man and I know the family. But far more, I know the God who peeled open tiles and steel girders so Dr. Lashley could peer through time and space into eternity. He did it because He loved him—and still does. Jesus Christ wasn't about to leave his servant and friend—or his family—believing a broken mind and body is the end of the story. Why?

Because a broken mind and body wasn't the end of His story; and He is absolutely committed to making sure it's not the end of yours.

As we'll discover, God never does anything without a good, loving purpose. That means the days we have left, filled with aches, pains, and prescriptions, where vigor abates and vitality is just a faded photograph, are just preparation for the ultimate expression of Love we're about to inherit. They are His promise that despite what we think and feel, an eternity of unending youthfulness is waiting for us just beyond the ceiling—and there is no way we're not going to get there.

That's counterintuitive, I know. It flies in the face of everything our present state of affairs says about what's ahead. Aging isn't for sissies and all that. But Jesus Christ doesn't care about the way things *look* or how the world views our decline. His only concern is for the way things *are*—from His perspective—which is the only one that counts. He wants us to trust old age—and it's ultimate expression, death—is nothing more than His progressively staging us for an eternity of youth we can't even imagine.

For that truth to sink in, way down deep where it should be, where the Lord cultivates conviction and hope and Satan can't tear it to pieces, we need time to deepen our understanding of The One making the promise. Otherwise, when doubts come (and they will) or one too many needle pricks tempt us to tell Him we want out of His program, we can withstand the assault, cling to the promise, and see the years ahead in a whole new light. We can treat them as He intends, a reminder of what's coming, a nod to what eyes of faith allow us to see: that when we wake up on the other side, we're going to discover there are no old people in heaven.

We commence with that end in mind—and there's no better place to start than, "In the beginning…"

GOD

GENESIS 1:1

Chapter 2

HE IS ... THE ONE

"Hear, O Israel! The Lord is our
God, the Lord is ONE!"

DEUTERONOMY 6:4, EMPHASIS MINE

He is the Greatest Person in the universe, the eternal Creator and Sustainer of all that exists, the expression of absolute, endless perfection, bound by no limitations of time, space, power, intellect, or depth of character. He is everywhere, all the time, meaning He does not divide—and therefore diminish—Himself in order to cover all the ground necessary to be present in and rule the universe and everything beyond it. Thus, He makes no distinction between a parsec (a unit of measure for large distances outside the solar system) and a Planck length (the shortest unit of length in space-time). There is no place all of Him is not (Genesis 1:1, Job 34:14-15, 36:4, 37:16, Psalm 90:2, 92:15, 139:7-10, 145:3, Proverbs 8:22-31, Isaiah 43:12-13, Matthew 5:48, Colossians 1:15-17, Revelation 4:11).

He is One, which means heaven is not a good 'ol boy network

that cobbled the universe together and runs it like a kangaroo court. He is One God, *the* Supreme Being. All powers and authorities exist at His discretion and serve to accomplish His purposes (Deuteronomy 4:35, 39, Job 42:2, Psalm 47:2, 83:18, 86:10, 90:4, 97:9, 103:19, Proverbs 16:4, 9, 21:1, Isaiah 41:12-26, 44:28, 45:1-7, 21-22, 46:9, Jeremiah 25:9, Habakkuk 1:5-11, 1 Peter 3:21-22). As One, His knowledge is organized in an eternally comprehensive, collective singularity, a function of His endless unity. It is instinctive, intuitive, spontaneous, and infused with eternally-depthless accuracy. He knows all things, for all time and beyond, all at once. There are no appendices, amendments, on-the-fly improvisations, or dangling participles of occurrence that catch Him by surprise or leave Him wondering what to do. Under His reign, everything that was, is, and will be is present and accounted for (1 Samuel 15:29, Psalm 147:5, Proverbs 33:16, Isaiah 40:28, 1 Corinthians 15:20-28, Revelation 1:17-18, 22:13).

There is nothing unrighteous or sinful in Him. His One supreme, unparalleled, unassailable, unending emotional and volitional core value is Love. It's not just *that* He loves. He *is* Love; its definition, source, sustainer, and ultimate, eternal expression. No part of His character, will, design, or purpose stands beyond it. All things—past, present, and future—even those desecrated by sin and marred by imperfection, have the expression of Love as their ultimate purpose (Genesis 50:20, Deuteronomy 8:16, Psalm 92:15, John 3:16, 7:18, Romans 8:28-39, 1 Corinthians 13:8-13, James 1:17, 1 John 4:8, 10, 16).

Permit one of many examples: Genesis 1:1 reads, "In the beginning, God created the heavens and the earth." Everything out of nothing, all that exists as a perfect, dynamic, four-dimensional portrait of what He's like and how He operates.

Read further and we discover a wrinkle. Some might call it an anomaly, an errant gene in the DNA of the universe. "The earth was formless and void," Genesis 1:2 says, "and darkness was over the surface of the deep, ..." Sounds like someone messed with the recipe. A perfect God does not create a world with one (pun intended) scintilla of darkness and void (i.e. lack of form; full of chaos and disorder). Does He?

Verse two continues. " ... and the Spirit of God was hovering (literally, "quivering" or "pulsating") over the surface of the waters." God's energetic, endless, loving Power and Perfection oscillated everywhere. He was fully aware and fully in charge. He'd foreseen the moment from the canyon rim of forever. "The Lord has made everything for its own purpose," His Spirit tells us, "even the wicked for the day of evil" (Proverbs 16:4).

What caused the darkness and void in the first place? I believe it was Satan's rebellion against God and banishment from heaven (Isaiah 14:12-20, Ezekiel 28:1-19, Luke 10:18). His position as the highest created being in the universe wasn't good enough. He wanted more. His greed and covetousness savaged his physical, moral, and intellectual beauty into its eternal opposite: perversion, mutiny, darkness, and death—fueled by a jealous hatred for God and His creation as strong today as the moment he was righteously thrown out. True to form, he unleashed his wrath on earth, mutilating it into something marred, squalid, and dark—just like him. It's what he does. Always. No exceptions.

Yet God was there, in the void and chaos when righteous angels shouted for joy over what He'd done (Job 38:4-7), pulsating life and perfection, rippling over the chaos and disorder like the star guiding the magi to Bethlehem. He had a plan, unified from before the beginning, to use Satan's hatred and disruption to further His greater purpose (again, see Proverbs 16:4). The God of Light and Life was about to demonstrate everyone and everything that's the antithesis of who He is and what He does is no match for His ferocious power and commitment to transform, renew, redeem, and restore.

So He said...

"Let there be..." light, sky and heaven, seas and dry land, vegetation, the sun, moon, and stars, life in the oceans and on land—all of it good (because there's no way it couldn't be), all of it brought into existence in perfect balance and harmony: light to illumine, life to fill, chaos gone. It was One to nothing, God.

In other words, His singularly perfect and endlessly unified Moral Character, Infinite Creativity, Boundless Love, and Limitless Power always coalesce to re-calibrate perfection from imperfection, bringing all things into harmony with Who He Is and how He operates. It's part-and-parcel of being One. The Holy Spirit chose the apostle Paul to express it like this:

> He made known to us the mystery of His will, according to His kind intention which He purposed in Him with a view to an administration suitable to the fullness of the times, that is, the summing up of all things in Christ, things in the heavens and things on the earth.
>
> EPHESIANS 1:9-10

Even sin and evil—as horribly offensive to His moral nature as they are—subserviently take their place in His Paradigm. That means your status as imperfect—its daily expressions in thought, word, or deed and its effect on your body and mind—have been permitted for a time so they can be redeemed for eternity.

The interim—where evil creates so much pain—tempts us to loathe Him for letting the dog off the leash. Yet we should take heart He has always seen sin as it *will* be: A dark, rabid mongrel chewing on the sofa leg of His universe, yes—but already kenneled in fire and darkness.

In God's view, sin and death are already dead. Satan, his demons, and unbelievers are in eternal hell. Every crime and sin committed by one human being against another has been justly dealt with. The discordant notes of His universe have resolved to make the melody of His Love endlessly full, eternally consistent, and ultimately breathtaking. All things. In all ways. Summed up, redeemed, and made perfect in Jesus Christ (Colossians 1:19-20). It was, is, and always will be God's way of doing things. All we have to do is wait to see what's been in His field of vision all along.

That redemption applies to our physical existence, which He illustrated with His own Flesh and Blood. Jesus Christ lived and died but was physically raised to life in glory to demonstrate He cannot be limited or held back by sin and death. His Word is clear He has every intention of sharing that experience with us (Psalm 16:8-11, Acts 2:24-28, Romans 6:5, 1 Corinthians 15:20-23, 42-50, Philippians 1:6, 3:20-21, Hebrews 11:39-40, 1 John 3:2).

Your journey there started when He became The One author of your life. He spooled you up from the micro world, appointing one of countless sperm to unite with one egg, two uniting then multiplying to become one—a reflection of His nature, endless diversity wrapped in complete unity.

Every cell division, every replication of your DNA, every specialized development of organ, bone, muscle, and sinew; every neuron, synapse, and neural pathway was carefully mapped and made by The Hand large and powerful enough to explode the universe into existence and throw a lightning bolt; yet small and delicate enough to enter the sub-atomic world and, like an artist busy about His masterpiece, make you, you (Job 36:32, Psalm 139:14-16, Isaiah 64:8).

Everything about you—from the color and texture of your hair, the size and shape of your features, the way you laugh, your natural inclinations, interests, and aptitudes—were "skillfully wrought in the depths of the earth" to quote Psalm 139:15, where your lack of awareness and His awareness of everything met in an indescribably complex fusion of power and powerlessness. It was the place where His hand attached you gently, just so, in just the right place on the placenta, where *The* Life used *a* life to give *you* life, until He was ready to unveil you to the world.

The details of His magnificent feat of engineering is the reason you can play the ivory off a keyboard but can't, for the life of you, throw a curveball; your best friend aces geometry and trig but struggles to write a paragraph; and your dad and brother can build or fix anything while you hyper-ventilate if they ask you to hand them a 3/8" socket.

His power and knowledge don't stop there. Every word, thought, and event of your life He foresaw before you were born (Psalm 139:1-6, 16). Daily, each and every second, He is busy overseeing *every* component of your existence, from the rate at which your white blood cells die off to the precise moment you reach the intersection of Main and Vine.

As the Holy Spirit reminds us, He will continue that work until every hint of sin and imperfection is gone—including bodies maligned and malformed with old age—because His ultimate purpose is for each of us to be a unique expression of His Son's perfection. Eternity would be incomplete without it.

Indeed, sustaining us eternally with thinning hair, bulging waistlines, and trifocals would be God wrapping His arms around sin and death and telling them "You got the best of Me. Nice job." Yet His Word thunders He did not allow His Son to undergo the decay of the grave; and as our Resurrection Forerunner, His experience will one day be ours (Psalm 16:10, 1 Corinthians 15:20, 35-57).

We want to believe everything we've just covered is true. But there's a lot in this world that argues against trusting God's claims about Himself and that He is committed to following through on what He says. If we're honest, sometimes the world's chaos and pain makes us wonder if it's all just a bunch of naïve, sugar-coated spin.

We need help and encouragement to hang onto the belief God is going to make us young again—and the best path there is aging and death. There's no shame in admitting it. There's also no shame in asking for page two of His resume. He is not angered or irritated by the request. He knows our fragilities (Psalm 103:14). He also knows information breeds confidence. He understands our fears about aging and death need to be ... Deep Sixed.

Chapter 3

DEEP SIXED

I hesitate to call Moses foolish. After all, he's one of the most well-known and beloved characters in the Bible.

But if the shoe fits...

How else should we describe a son of ancient Egyptian royalty who, having tasted the fruit of its luxury and power, tossed it aside like a grape stem for the stench and dry dust of sheep herding in the Sinai desert? One minute, the wealth and privilege of Egypt as far as the eye could see. The next, he was brushing scorpions off rocks and thinking "Hell's gate has to be around here somewhere."

What happened? In one rash, ill-conceived moment of vengeance, he murdered an Egyptian for mistreating a Jew and ran for his life into some of the most God (not)-forsaken wilderness on the face of the earth.

He spent the next four *decades* thinking about it. Fourteen thousand six hundred days that reminded him of what irrational anger does, what he'd given up, and what he'd become: a washed-up has-been who traded an Egyptian scepter for a shepherd's staff. Way to go, Moses.

Conventional thinking wouldn't peg someone like that for one of the most important jobs in history. Then again, God is not bound by conventional thinking—especially when it comes to measuring value by merit. So He chose a fool and a murderer to lead the nation of Israel out of Egypt after 430 years of slavery; and to be the one to whom He'd reveal His heart and Holy Word. A felon given the Words of Life. Only God would come up with that.

If you're familiar with the Bible, you might think the Words of Life I'm referring to are the Ten Commandments … but they're not.

They are important to be sure, God's revelation of truth and conduct written by His finger on tablets of stone (Exodus 31:18). They are holy, righteous, and just—at first glance, the perfect, unblemished blueprint for how to live with Him and each other. But a deeper look reveals they had another equally important purpose.

That became evident when God's people quickly gave in to sinful impulses after hearing God declare the Ten Commandments. They'd seen His power through plagues in Egypt and the Egyptian army drowned in the Red Sea. Now they were at the base of Mt. Sinai, completely overwhelmed as His voice literally thundered in glory and power. It's why they asked *Moses* to speak with Him, fearing if they heard His voice again they would die (Exodus 19:17-20:19). Moses obliged and went to the top of the mountain.

Forty days later, no Moses. Moses must be gone. Maybe he fell off a cliff. Maybe he said something God didn't like and the Lord swatted him like a housefly. Regardless, God's people were apparently on their own—and did what people do when they figure God and His spokesmen aren't around. They made their own god and had a massive party to celebrate. So much for their pledge days earlier that "All the Lord has spoken we will do" and His command "You shall have no other gods before Me" (Exodus

19:8, 24:3, 20:3). Slightly more than a month is all it took to show the Ten Commandments are an impossible standard to keep.

In the centuries that followed Old Testament writers led by His Spirit echoed that truth. One has only to read 1 Kings 8:46, Job 25:1-6, Psalm 14:1-3, Ecclesiastes 7:20, or Isaiah 64:6 to get it. No man, no woman, no child, no matter how righteous they seem, has the capacity to live the Ten Commandments perfectly every hour, every day of their lives. No exceptions. Yes, the Ten Commandments reveal how we are supposed to live with God and each other. They also the reveal how we *can't* live and why we need a Savior (Romans 7:10-12, Romans 5:20-21, 7:24-25, Galatians 3:21-26).

The Ten Commandments, then, are not the words of life mentioned a moment ago. Those words are the revelation of God's true nature and character, shared with His people *after* their devastating sin. They provide a behind-the-scenes look at the *heart* of the Person who authored the Ten Commandments.

Here's the context: God promised He would take His people to Canaan, settle them there, and if they remained faithful, bless them. Despite their having made a golden calf their god, He had every intention of fulfilling His end of the bargain. It's the way He is. Always faithful. Always true. Always trustworthy. Even when we're not.

He told Moses He'd send an angel with them to provide safe passage, which left Moses restless and unsettled. God was his Friend; they talked face-to-face (Exodus 33:1-11). It was a bond Moses had with no one else. The thought of leading two million people through the desert without his Best Friend hit him in the face like a blinding sandstorm. Angels are great and powerful, to be sure. But they're not God.

Moses put on his big boy underpants and got bold. He asked his Friend to go with them, which might seem like he was pushing it. God could have easily thought, "Good... *GRIEF!!!* I hauled him out of exile, made him a great leader, and we just finished forty days of prime time together. Now he expects me to hang with a crowd whose faithfulness evaporates like the morning fog. Is this guy *never* satisfied?... Maybe I will use that flyswatter." But that's making God out to be just another human being and He is anything but. He did what He does. He was gracious. He honored Moses' request (Exodus 33:12-17).

Moses wasn't done. "I pray You," he said, "Show me Your glory!" (Exodus 33:18). He was asking God to show him what He's *really* like, to peel away his assumptions and sear a portrait of His character into Moses' mind and heart that would not go away. His success depended on it.

Without hesitation, God agreed. He told Moses to meet him on Mount Sinai the next morning. Here's what happened:

> The LORD descended in the cloud and stood there with him as he called upon the name of the LORD. Then the LORD passed by in front of him and proclaimed, "The LORD, the LORD God, compassionate and gracious, slow to anger, and abounding in lovingkindness and truth; Who keeps lovingkindness for thousands, Who forgives iniquity, transgression and sin; yet He will by no means leave *the guilty* unpunished, visiting the iniquity of fathers on the children and on the grandchildren to the third and fourth generations."
>
> Exodus 34:6-7

Wow.

If you hadn't noticed, human beings tend toward the negative. Sorry to say, we often *like* it. The nightly news is a euphemism for bad news. We love hearing how the bad guy got what was coming to him; and if someone does something we don't like or understand, we script negative stories about their motives and heart. It's how we roll.

We need to be careful about doing the same here. Our tendency is to go to the end of verse seven first—the part about the guilty being punished and its trickle-down effect to our great-grandchildren. We assume—as the enemy of our souls wants us to—it's the major description of God's character. Vehement. Angry. A God keeping track of sins who CAN'T WAIT to pounce—not only on us but innocent descendants two generations off.

I guess all the other stuff at the beginning of verse six is just window dressing, divinely-ordained spin to keep our eyes off the real truth.

Right?

No. That's not right. God does not stutter. He doesn't misspeak, misconstrue, or misdirect. He doesn't mess up the order of what He wants to say. 'B' follows 'A,' not the reverse. The first thing is the most important thing; it comes before and directs everything else.

It's no mistake, then, that the first thing He declared as He walked right by His friend was His name: "The Lord," ("Yahweh," "I AM WHO I AM") the verbal and auditory symbol summing up His character and nature, the same name He used when Moses met Him in Exodus 3. He followed it with a declaration of His position ("the Lord God"), the Supreme, Eternal Being (discussed in chapter two).

With those things in tow, He left Moses awash in the only other thing which mattered: the declaration of six character traits that swept over him like a tidal wave, leaving no doubt about what His Best Friend is like.

He is compassionate. He is intimately acquainted with all our ways, infinitely aware of the way sin pollutes us as a race and as individuals—and customizes His loving actions and responses on our behalf in accordance with that knowledge (Psalm 33:14-15, 103:14, 139:1-4).

He is gracious. For those related to Him by faith in His Son, He forgives all our sins—past, present, and future. The Bible says He tosses them in the depths of the sea and separates us from their eternal penalty as far as the east is from the west. He does not treat us as our sins deserve but views us as perfect, just as His Son in whom we trust is perfect (Nehemiah 9:31, Psalm 103:6-14, 130:3-4, 145:8, Micah 7:18-20, Romans 4:5, 5:18, 2 Corinthians 5:21, Galatians 3:26-27).

He is slow to anger, meaning He is patient. Incredibly patient. The Bible tells us His tolerance of sin isn't marked by hours, days, months, or years. He's willing to wait centuries for a nation and decades for a person. He beckons all to return to The One Who Loves them more than they know, Who wants to care for them as no one else can, Who takes absolutely no pleasure in the death of the wicked but would much rather they turn from their sin, return to Him, and live. It's the same patience which stays His hand from drawing the curtain on this age and exercising His wrath against sin. He wants everyone to have every chance possible to be saved from His eternal judgment (Psalm 145:8, Jeremiah 18:7-8, Ezekiel 18:21-23, 32, Joel 2:12-13, Jonah 4:2, Luke 13:34, Romans 9:22-23, 1 Timothy 2:4, 2 Peter 3:9).

He abounds in loyal love that is not dependent on the imperfect love we return to Him. He remains faithful even when we live by sight rather than faith and inevitably mess things up. He is kind, not jealous; does not brag and is not arrogant; does not act in an unbecoming or self-serving way; never allows anger to be a knee-jerk reaction for having been offended, made fun of, or ignored; doesn't rejoice in unrighteousness but in the truth; puts up with all things, hopes all things, and endures all things (Deuteronomy 7:9, 2 Chronicles 7:3, 6, 20:21, Psalm 57:9-10, 86:5, 100:5, 136:1-26, Isaiah 49:14-16, John 3:16, 1 Corinthians 13:1-13, Ephesians 2:4-5).

All His paths, as Psalm 25:10 says, are lovingkindness and truth. Everything He does, every movement around every preon and lepton, quasar and black hole, and every action taken in the affairs of men, whether it's to control the rise and fall of nations or plant a gentle impulse in the human heart, is perfectly nuanced by a commitment to act with loyal love (and truth, see below) toward those who fear Him (Psalms 33:4, 34:7, 103:11, Proverbs 16:33, 21:1, Isaiah 40:21-26).

His love compelled God the Son, Jesus Christ, to voluntarily leave the glory of heaven, come here as our Servant, and offer Himself as a ransom for sin by humbling Himself to the point of death on a Cross; only be to be exalted to heaven by God the Father. There, He serves as our compassionate, gracious Advocate, working in concert with the Holy Spirit to reveal truth, enable our lives with His power, and shape our prayers in accordance with the Father's will; and commissions angels to render service to us during our time on earth. In short, it's a Love that will never fall short of love's ultimate expression. As we said before, God doesn't *just* love. He *is* Love (Mark 10:45, Acts 1:9-11, Romans 8:26-27, 34, Philippians 2:6-8, Hebrews 1:13-14, 2:17, 4:14-16, 7:25, 1 John 2:1, 4:8-10).

He is Truth, the eternal, boundless demarcation of facts which describe and express His character, nature, and universe (and all things beyond it)—and the infinite antithesis of Satan, in whom there is no truth. All math, all science, all insinuations and textures of psyche and soul which are pure reality and not theorized imaginings of fallible human intellect or insight, reside in Him and emanate from Him. There is no truth that is truth that's not His truth (2 Samuel 7:28, Psalm 19:7-14, 31:5, 111:7, 119:151, 160, John 8:44, 17:17, Ephesians 4:21, Colossians 2:2-3, 1 John 5:6). And,

He forgives iniquity, transgression, and sin. Please note the threefold description. It's there for emphasis to let us know our wrongdoing—regardless of how heinous or despicable, how long it's gone on, the ways it's expressed itself, or how many people we've hurt—will be forgiven in a way unmatched by any other Person. Total. Complete. Eternal. Just like Him (John 3:16, 5:24, Romans 6:10, 23, Hebrews 10:12-18, 1 Peter 3:18).

Does justice belong with His compassion, grace, patience, loyal love, and truth? Yes. Those injured by sin must be vindicated (including punishment for those who've wronged them) something rule-of-law societies recognize, albeit imperfectly. It's why God included it in His self-disclosure to Moses.

But it's important to understand God was not telling Moses—and is not telling us—innocent descendants suffer judgment for things they didn't do (Ezekiel 18:14-20). He's simply acknowledging He'll deal with descendants who follow in their ancestors' sinful footsteps in His time and His way (as He said He'd do with the disobedient generation of Moses' day, see Exodus 32:31-35).

Moses was ridin' herd on two million people trekking to the Promised Land and needed to know more about the Trail Boss. God let him know. After all, "a friend loves at all times and a brother is born for adversity" (Proverbs 17:17) and God was Moses' friend. Centuries later David, king of Israel, learned about the Trail Boss, too.

> Even though I walk through the valley of the shadow of death, I fear no evil, for You are with me; Your rod and Your staff, they comfort me. You prepare a table before me in the presence of my enemies; You have anointed my head with oil; my cup overflows. Surely goodness and lovingkindness will follow me all the days of my life, and I will dwell in the house of the LORD forever.
>
> PSALM 23:4-6

"The valley of the shadow of death." Moses eventually walked it. So did David. Even the Lord, in His humanity, did. You and I will, too. All three learned everything God says and does is an expression of His character, which never changes, *even when death is near.*

No exceptions. Ever.

They were, in essence, Deep Sixed, immersed in the six-point declaration and experience of God's character so real and vibrant there was no mistaking Who He Is and What He's like. If you and I are to walk that valley and discover the joy on the other side, what it means to truly "dwell in the house of the Lord forever," to live in the place where the only thing that dies is old age, our fears about growing old need to be dropped in the grave and Deep-sixed, too. They need to be replaced with absolute confidence

His declaration of character applies everywhere, all the time, to those whose faith rests in Him, no matter what the circumstance. We need to understand believing what He says about Himself gives us confidence to accept diminishing youth here in preparation for its full embrace there. We need faith in One Truth, comprised of six distinct yet indivisible truths, that feeble hands and wobbly legs can steady themselves on when diminished minds and bodies try to convince us what we once had we will never have again.

The Deep Six, with their youth-filled hopefulness and vigor, exploding from The Ageless God Who created and will restore ageless Man, should always remind and comfort us that when it comes to our final years here, His promise is we're not getting old; we're getting ready. Ready to be what we were created to be, bereft of imperfection and exploding with every possible combination, iteration, composition, meld, mixture, and synthesis of physical, intellectual, psychological, and spiritual flawlessness. The perfect version of you. And me. With Him. Forever.

How's that for a retirement plan, Mr. Broker Man?

Now we have a clear bead on what God is like. With Him at life's helm, steering by the north star of the Deep Six, we can trust He knows what He's doing, even when He sails us into the stormy waters of old age.

He knows it's hard to trust Him. It's why He's given us landmarks and lighthouses to keep our bearings; rock solid biblical truths that don't shatter in turbulence or float off like driftwood; helping us see what's real and what's just an illusion so we can keep the shoreline of eternal youthfulness in sight.

He knows how to get us there. One might say He knows the journey like the back of His omnipotent, nail-pierced Hands. One could hardly blame Him for telling us to relax and leave the details to Him.

But He is compassionate, remember? He knows how fragile our fragilities are. He knows Truth is important. It comforts and strengthens us which is what He wants to do. It's why, to borrow a picture from a frantic scene on the Sea of Galilee long ago, He invites us to step out of the boat and walk around in the storm with Him (Matthew 14:22-33). All we need to do is keep our eyes on Him and listen to what He says. We'll see what's True about aging and death—and what lies we can toss aside like piles of rotting kelp.

So what do you say we step out there with Him? We're going to die anyway so there's nothing to lose, right? It might as well be hanging on to Him while lies about old age slip through our fingers...

Chapter 4

IT'S ALL ABOUT IMAGE

We humans are a curious lot.

We're afraid of heights but fly in airplanes. We savor aged wine but sour on old milk. We hate mold in the bathroom but love it in our blue cheese. We describe water as hard and soft when really, it's just wet.

We call north "up" and south "down" when it's obvious to anyone the sky is "up" and the ground is "down." Rainy days get us down but we're down when we haven't had enough rain. Dirt is good in the flower bed but bad on the living room floor. We fish for bass, play bass, and run the bases. If we're diggin' it we either like it or we're attacking it with a shovel. We love cool people and can be cool with it; but don't ask us to warm to someone who's cold. We pronounce "colonel," "kernel." Canine halitosis? No problem. Our mug goes right in the dog's face anyway, knowing full-well where that oral cavity has been. Totally different reaction if the *mauvaise odeur* belongs to Aunt Maude.

Ample brain power means we're smart; but it smarts when we stub our toe. We love shade on a summer day but think of the nefarious as "shady." We can vacuum a rug, wear a rug, or cut a rug. Gas is fuel but when exhausted, we're gassed. Somehow, someway, agreeing with something, being savvy about it, or acceptance by the in-crowd is equated with the area of human anatomy where the femur has a meet-and-greet with the pelvis. Go figure.

Most relevant to our topic, when it comes to furniture, we honor and value antiques. Yet when it comes to our bodies and appearance, it's the last word we want to hear. A show of hands from anyone who believes, "Sarah, your face is such an *antique*" is a compliment?

Which leads to the question, "Why are we so obsessed with staying young?" Why spend billions on cosmetic surgery, gym memberships, and free testosterone? Why do job recruiters overlook people over fifty-five? Why is retirement-age advertising just as likely to show sixty-something hipsters enjoying life to the fullest as those who've fallen and can't get up?

Why? Youth is king. Youth is glamor. Youth is humanity at its best. It's an inalienable right, alongside life, liberty, and the pursuit of happiness. For many, it *is* the pursuit of happiness.

It's also time-bound and limited to a few fleeting years between puberty and love handles. Which raises another question.

Why is it so important we spin our age so the reverse of what's happening is the focus? Why is aging such a big deal? It happens. It's going to happen. It's going to keep happening. The tight abs of our twenties *will* give way to the swinging triceps of our seventies and eighties. Our energy will abate. Our eyesight will weaken. Our hearing will diminish. Our children will tire of hearing the same question over and over again. Cataracts and catheters will sometimes be a matching set.

Solomon, a man of unparalleled biblical wisdom, expressed that truth very elegantly in Ecclesiastes 12:1-8. It's too lengthy to quote here but well worth a moment to read. Please. Feel free. I'm in no hurry. I've got to check if I took my blood thinner this morning, anyway. I can't remember.

—✳—

Solomon had his arms around more of the accoutrements of youth—success, power, wealth, and pleasure—than most can imagine (see Ecclesiastes 2:1-11). But as we see in Ecclesiastes 12, he learned he couldn't hang onto it. Youth, with all its promise and passion, is fleeting. We can dread that all we want. We can nip-tuck it into the corner or stave it off with supplements—ultimately, to no avail. It's going to happen—and with good reason.

Two reasons, actually. And contrary to the world's perspective, they tip us off something far better is on the horizon. I trust it doesn't surprise anyone we find them in the opening pages of the *Old* Testament.

WE ARE IMAGE BEARERS

If you're at all familiar with the first chapter of Genesis you know a key concept in creation is Man made in God's image (v. 27). Theologians call that the *imago dei* (Latin for "image of God") and have waxed eloquent for centuries on its implications: While we are not gods, we have god-like qualities like a moral sense, an awareness of the spiritual, an ability to relate to Him and each other, a free will, the knowledge of good and evil, and are commissioned to serve Him as vice-regents over creation. They've paid less attention to how our appearance conveys that image.

When Adam was formed from the dust of the ground—and

Eve fashioned from his rib—they were physically designed to fulfill their role as perfect image bearers. They not only acted like God—they looked like Him, too. Genesis 3:8 provides a glimpse: After Adam and Eve sinned, "they heard the sound of the Lord God walking in the garden in the cool of the day." Branches rustled. Birds took flight. Swirling eddies of glory behind and before signaled God was on the move.

We don't know if He looked like the glorified man Ezekiel, Daniel, and the apostle John saw (Ezekiel 1:26-28, 8:2, Daniel 3:25, 7:13-14, Revelation 1:12-16), revealed only His feet or back as was the case with Moses and the seventy elders of Israel (Exodus 24:9-11, 33:21-23, 34:6-7), appeared in the subdued form beheld by Abraham, Jacob, Joshua, and Samson's parents (Genesis 18:1-33, Genesis 32:24-32, Joshua 5:13-15, Judges 13:1-23), or was personified in a way for which there's no biblical parallel. All we know is He was walking—and He chose male and female humans as the perfect representation of His presence so their fellowship with Him would be whole and complete (Genesis 1:27, 2:18-25).

But perfect humanity faltered. Horribly. Adam and Eve's choice to disobey God and listen to Satan's lies marred their ability to reflect everything about their Creator—including His physical appearance. That didn't just apply to square shoulders and high cheek bones. It affected their physiology, neurology, and psychology, too. Their bodies were suddenly flawed, their neurons started misfiring, their frame of mind was altered, and their fellowship with God was broken. It's why when they heard Him, they did what sinners always do: they hid, afraid He'd see sin had ravaged perfection (Genesis 3:8-10).

It did, true enough.

But it didn't *erase* it.

It couldn't. God was still there, on the move—just as when the world was formless and void and darkness was over the surface of the deep (Genesis 1:2). As was the case then, He invaded chaos with grace—and in the first act to indicate Christ would one day take care of what sin had done—shed the blood of an animal to clothe those He loved. That is, He covered their shame and naked imperfection (Genesis 3:21).

Notice the difference: God acknowledged their sin and sacrificed to *cover it*—meaning, "to pay its penalty." They tried to *cover it up*, no doubt hoping to regain ageless perfection. Sound familiar?

Their children learned the technique well. When their son Cain's jealousy over his brother Abel's sacrifice erupted into murder and a cover-up, God asked him, "Where is Abel your brother?" Abel's famous response was, "I do not know. Am I my brother's keeper?" (Genesis 4:9).

But Cain did know—and knew he'd sinned. Just like his parents, he tried to bury the truth—literally. Sin seized the beauty of the *imago dei* ("image of God") and made a sick, twisted version of it. The job now was to spin falsehood into truth (and vice-versa) and prop it up as the enduring image. Human beings have been at that game ever since.

We can't help it. Projecting an image is deeply embedded in our DNA. It's what we were made to do—but His way. Without Him, everyone we meet, every person we interact with, every situation we find ourselves in is about projecting an illusion. We want to be what we are not. We *must* be because we can't face what we truly are. It grates against the *imago dei*. If we can't have it legitimately, we'll maneuver and manipulate until the falsehood becomes reality (or at least we think it does).

Our bodies are a prime billboard for that illusion. We sculpt, paint, tattoo, liposuck, and exercise them into shapes and images that, in our mind at least, project the air of perfection, of what we once had in the Garden. Blend in a bit of self-generated knowledge, a pinch of self-ordained wisdom, a smattering of hipness, and voila! I am who I AM made me to be.

It's a fool's errand for two reasons.

First, it falls prey to the belief our image is up to us. That means we doubt that when He forgives us He also recreates us, instantly pegging the meter of who we are to read "perfect" (2 Corinthians 5:17). Too many of us believe He is so disgusted and inflamed by our wrongdoing He can't possibly see us as anything but wretched and horrible.

That's exactly what Satan wants us to think. He wants us to misunderstand the depth of God's generosity and compassion. He convinced Adam and Eve God wasn't as good as they thought (Genesis 3:1-5). He and his henchmen have been selling that snake oil ever since—and pressuring us, on our own, to make up the difference.

But is that what He's like? Did He react to Adam and Eve with bitter disgust and rejection? Where does Genesis 3 say that? Yes, He was honest about what they'd done and the consequences which followed—but He also promised one day He'd defeat Satan (3:15); provide for them in the meantime (3:21); and protect them from living in their sinful state forever (3:22-24).

And what of the ultimate expression of God's heart in Jesus Christ? He is The Sinless One who *became our sin* so we could become "the righteousness of God in Him." That means God the Father sees us as He sees His Son: perfectly righteous, perfectly just, perfectly perfect, just like He saw Adam and Eve before they sinned (2 Corinthians 5:21).

Second, because we fail to understand that—and make no

mistake, most people (including Christians) don't—we go to extraordinary lengths and employ whatever means necessary to get *other people* to affirm our image. It's why facts are changed, kingdoms are built, monuments erected, companies created, and Halls of Fame constructed. It's why album covers look cool and stars demand hours be spent setting up the shot. It's the lifeblood of social media, the fuel of the job search, and the language of champions. "Image, image, image. I'm special. I'm the best. I need *you* to like and affirm *me*."

Yet we were never made to do that for each other. God is far too kind than to foist the burden for our self-worth on someone who isn't perfect. It's not fair to them and it's not fair to us. *He* created our image. *He* has the desire and ability to sustain it— and is the only One who can. Seeking it from others drives us to manipulate them—which cheapens them, weakens us, and minimizes God. No one wins.

God is the only One Who can redeem our image—including our bodies. Who better to do it than the Perfect One? Indeed, He *wants* to—and we need look no further than the empty tomb for proof. Sin and death couldn't eternally decimate the body of Jesus Christ—and He will not let it eternally pillage ours. His resurrection body is a down payment on our own (1 Corinthians 15:22-23).

All things. In all ways. Summed up, redeemed, and made perfect in Him, remember?

HAS ANYONE SEEN MY OLD FRIEND METHUSELAH?

Immediately after the account of Cain and Abel in Genesis 4, the Holy Spirit shows us how long people lived (Genesis 5).

Adam was 930 when he died; his son, Seth was 912. Seth's son, Enosh was 905. Continue reading to verse 27 and you'll discover Methuselah was 969.

That's no mistake. God is artfully weaving redemption into the story of sin. He made this world. It's His. We marred it. He wants it back—He wants us back, the way we were, before Satan encroached and we foolishly gave in. It doesn't matter to Him it was—and continues to be—our fault. He's moving in history to correct what we did through what only He can do. It's why Genesis 5 follows Genesis 4. *In God's story, life follows death.*

True, everyone in Genesis 5 died (except Enoch). But their age demonstrated they were still infused with the remnants of eternal youth. It is a reminder of what was and will be again, that before sin entered our reality, there was no age. No growing old. No terminal diagnoses. No abated energy or diminished physical, intellectual, or emotional prowess. We were perfect. Perfectly formed. Perfectly functional. Perfectly *young.*

Indeed, we hate aging because deep in the human soul, one we share collectively and bear individually, we *know* we weren't made to die. He made us to live, with Him, without flaw, forever. Sadly, most of the world careens wildly through life believing procedures, vitamins, diets, and workouts are the way to steal agelessness from age, living scared all the way to death it's a heist they'll never pull off.

Without Him, they won't—which gives, "I am the Way, the Truth, and the Life; no one comes to the Father but through Me" ultimate meaning (John 14:6). Jesus Christ conquered sin and death through the cross and resurrection. It qualifies Him to turn the Garden of Gethsemane into the Garden of Eden again, the place of sin and sorrow into a perfect paradise, so we can have with Him what we had when the world was … *young.*

Faith in Him means our restoration into ageless, physical perfection is assured. We'll leave this place and join Him to fully experience what it means to have our bodies (which He describes as a temple of the Holy Spirit) fully restored: Perfect temples of the Spirit perfectly redeemed, perfectly united, perfectly dwelling with The One True Temple (John 2:15-21, 17:11, 22, 1 Corinthians 3:16, 6:19, 2 Corinthians 5:1-5). That's why there aren't any old people in heaven. It's why there can't be.

But old ways of thinking die hard. It's difficult to look in the mirror at wrinkles and sags and blow out more birthday candles than ever and not believe what's lost is gone forever. Decades in a world of decay does that to us. It can and often does decimate hope—especially when we're surrounded by constant reminders of life's "D words."

BUCKET LISTS,
BRASS RINGS, AND
"I SURE WISH I HAD ..."

R emember seventeen?
Not the magazine.

The age.

I do. I don't know how much longer I will but for now, the memories are intact. Whiskers were overtaking acne. A new sense of self, of what it meant to be a man, was breaking through the eggshell of my adolescence. Painful, debilitating shyness, especially around girls, wasn't as acute. I could say "hi" to them in the hallway. I could ask one to dance. I could even call for a date without spending two days mustering enough courage to pick up the phone and dial her number.

(If you're wondering what "dialing" a number means, you're probably too young for this book. But feel free to ask your dad or grandad. They can tell you; along with tall tales of rabbit ears on televisions and shag carpeting. Then come back here when you and your friends start discussing "things heading south"—with no reference to compass points intended).

Seventeen was also the time when my height and weight were gaining ground on my age. To put that in perspective, at fourteen, I was 5'4," 115 pounds, soakin' wet. I also had a nice set of tortoise shell glasses to go with that all-world physique.

I know. You don't have to say it. I was mayor of Nerdsville.

By eighteen, I'd grown eight inches and gained fifty pounds. I wasn't a shrimp anymore. Maybe there *was* a place of respectability out there for me. I started thinking about my future—the one beyond the diploma, the one college promised, a life outside the oppressive regime of the high school hallway (where status was all about athletic conquests or how cool others thought you were), the place where freedom shook hands with opportunity, where insecurity died and confidence came to life. Dreams were made out there—and if I needed a boost, a place to take shelter from the occasional storm that blew up or just needed a taste of Mom's cooking, home would be just a phone call or (in my case) a two-hour plane ride away.

The privileges of married life were on my mind, too. Companionship and intimacy, the two great pillars of adulthood, loomed closer than ever. God created me for it. My mind, body, and spirit were drawing closer to the mature frame that would enable me to build a life on that foundation. It would be good. It would be godly. It would be awesome. All systems were "go." The dream and hope were alive.

———

Imagine another young man around seventeen, his voice cracking with the same exuberant idealism. Most of life's goodness is still ahead. One day soon, he'll embrace his life-long lover and build a life worth remembering. He accelerates down life's runway, takeoff thrust set and airspeed alive, and rotates toward the hope and the dream. It is going to be good. It is going to be godly. It is going to be awesome. All systems are "go" for him, too.

Then without warning, he loses power, banks sharply, and nose-dives toward the ground. The vertigo is staggering. Stumbling out of the wreckage, a quick look around reveals he's been forc-ibly removed from the royal family in which he was raised and transported almost 1,700 miles to a land and culture as alien as a Mars landscape. The language is gibberish and Mom's linguini is a memory. Imagine further his first introduction to hometown hos-pitality could well have been a court-appointed 'clinician' tasked with removing the twin towers of his manhood.[1]

So much for life's bucket list. So much for the brass ring of dreams hanging around his heart like a prizefighter's champion-ship belt. So much for enjoying all the benefits of the way God made him. The Song of Solomon would remain just words on a page. Welcome to Babylon, Daniel, son of Judah. Here is your new life, disappointments and all. And oh by the way…

You will never see home again.

If only Daniel was an isolated example. You and I know he's not. The Bible tells of others whose bucket lists and brass rings also melted in the dross of a sinful world. As mentioned earlier in the book, Adam and Eve watched perfection slip from their grasp—with no one to blame but themselves. Moses yearned to see the

---

1. I'm indebted to Christopher R. Smith at https://goodquestionblog.com/2014/05/28/were-daniel-and-his-friends-eunuchs/ for insights regarding Daniel being made a eunuch.

Promised Land. But one rash act—a moment when sin got the best of him, when He misrepresented God as angry with His people when He wasn't—brought the loss of that privilege. The best he would have is a view of the land from a distant mountaintop (Numbers 20:1-13, Deuteronomy 34:1-5).

Naomi left Bethlehem for the promise of a better life in the land of Moab, only to bury those dreams in the graves of her husband and two sons. Upon returning home, she told everyone to call her "Mara" (meaning "bitter") "for the Almighty has dealt very bitterly with me. I went out full but the Lord has brought me back empty..." (Ruth 1:20-21).

Jeremiah's ministry was laced with ridicule, opposition, mistreatment, and hardship culminating in forced exile in Egypt. Like Daniel, he would never see home again (Jeremiah 7:27, 37-38:6, 43:1-7). The apostle Paul gave up the brass ring of his rank as a "Hebrew of Hebrews," (which means his peers thought he followed the Mosaic Law flawlessly, Philippians 3:4-6) for the hardship of life on the road as a servant of Christ (1 Corinthians 9:-1-12, 2 Corinthians 4:7-12, 11:23-33).

Above them all, Jesus Christ relinquished heavenly glory to come here as the quintessential servant, offering Himself as the ultimate ransom for our sins. It required obedience to the point of an excruciating death He begged His Father He could avoid (Matthew 26:39, Mark 10:45, Philippians 2:6-8).

But God The Father had other plans.

Experiences like these are ones for which we have an abundant list of "D" words: disappointment, disillusionment, dissatisfaction, depression, disenchantment, dejection, despondency, and dismay. We describe someone dealing with such things as discontent, disconsolate, distressed, doleful, in despair, down in the dumps, or in the doldrums. Add in misfortune, setback, chagrin, feeling crestfallen, moping about, going through a letdown, and feeling gloomy and well... you get it.

The malaise isn't common. It's epidemic. It know no bounds, is no respecter of persons, status, or station-in-life. It can strike without warning, snarling lives and emotions like a bird's nest on a fishing rod. It cares nothing for convenience or the hassles we're dealing with. It loves to pile on—and stay on. The more, the more miserable; misery loves company.

Collectively, the "D" words describe the root symptom of the world's sins and imperfections. They are the emotional synonyms of unmet expectations. Things don't go as we hope. We're not respected. Our privacy is ignored. Our just due is cast aside. What is rightfully ours is unfairly—and at times, violently—taken. The person we expect to be faithful, competent, or unselfish, isn't. Someone doesn't do—or something doesn't go—as expected, and the "D" words rush in like a tsunami.

That's only half of it. Equally pervasive is an endlessly irritating thought running around our mind like a demon-possessed race car. Its piercing, high-pitched approach and wailing departure—lap after relentless lap—is a reminder few of us live the life we imagined.[2] It's captured in five words which don't comprise a sentence but can constitute a lifetime; the phrase everyone knows and wishes we could forget:

"I sure wish I had..."

For purposes here, let's dispense with regrets over sin. We're

---

2. Thanks to pastor and friend, Bob Sheffield, for this phrasing.

old enough to know the pain of sin is inversely proportional to the pleasure it promises. We'd all love a do-over. Yet we can reach out for Him in confession and repentance, knowing the promise of eternal forgiveness displayed in the lives David, Manasseh, Peter, and Paul can be ours, too (2 Samuel 11-12, 2 Chronicles 33:1-13, Psalm 32, 51, Isaiah 55:7, Ezekiel 18:21-22 and vv. 27-28, Luke 22:31-34, 54-62, John 10:28, 21:15-17, Acts 9:1-18, 1 Timothy 1:12-17, 1 John 1:9). All things. In all ways. Summed up, redeemed, and made perfect in Him.

No, the focus here is on talents and opportunities we never followed through on or were too afraid to pursue. Do you wish you had…

Accepted the scholarship? Become a carpenter? Pursued engineering? Taken piano? Gone to flight school? Patented that invention? Signed up for art class? Founded a non-profit? Opened a floral shop? Worked with children? Followed through on ballet? Attended seminary? Become a sonographer? Worked as a park ranger? Written a book? Composed a song? Stayed with gymnastics?

Gone into software design? Become a chef, nurse, teacher, jeweler, paramedic, project manager, coach, or constitutional attorney? Pursued photography? Explored law enforcement? Stayed in the military? Gotten out of the military? Become a veterinarian? Finished med school? Learned equine therapy? Pursued dentistry? Worked on a ranch? Become a tower crane operator? An architect? Pursued what you were good at instead of a paycheck?

Is it any wonder we're all about bucket lists and brass rings? Life commits far too much not-so-petty larceny, depriving us of things, people, opportunities, and experiences we're convinced would have enriched us or made use of the way God made us. It's why so many in our world are of the mindset we need to do *everything* we can to take back *as much* as we can.

To make matters worse, we get one crack at making up the difference. One. One chance to experience, one chance to know, one chance to see, hear, smell, taste, and touch. Thai beaches, the Champs-Élysées, Broadway, and the Great Barrier Reef aren't going anywhere—but they can't come to us, either. It's why we make airplanes. *Carpe diem* everyone. We only live once, right? Right?

Well... not exactly. In fact, not at all.

We only live once *here.*

Too often, we lose sight of that, living as if bucket lists and brass rings really are the last best hope for a life of meaning and joy. Fortunately, Jesus Christ has a clearer field of vision. He knows there is another place, more real than anything we've known here. He is committed to getting us ready for it. Right now, as you read this, He is busy preparing a place there especially designed for *you.* Which means He is equally busy preparing *you* for that new place—which has no room for imperfect human beings. We'd mess it up sure as the imperfect nose on my imperfect face; which means when it comes to getting us ready for the future there is some... dismantling required.

Chapter 6

SOME DISMANTLING REQUIRED

Part One

It's just never good enough, is it?

Cars, electronic devices, sports stadiums, wardrobes, jobs, dream homes—if we can design it, build it, name it, see it, sew it, touch it, play it, play with it, buy it, sell it, fly it; walk in, on, around or through it; travel to it or work at it—we'll find something wrong with it. It's what we do.

New becomes old the minute it's new. Metal rusts, pipes crack, circuits degrade, romance fades. Fads change, tires wear, roofs leak, and knees give out. Last year's model yields to this year's faster, sleeker version. The song we thought we'd never tire of is suddenly off our playlist. We can't remember who won the biggest sporting event in human history three months ago.

No worries. That's all yesterday's news. Something better and a cut above is right around the corner. It has to be—proof positive the human heart has been, is, and always will be on a relentless search to find the next best thing.

It may surprise you I'm only going to spend one sentence's worth of your time and my penmanship to note there's a lot wrong with that.

There. I said it. That's that.

It may also surprise you I'm here to help us see the drive to dismantle and discard for the next best thing is an important part of how God made us. More to the point, it's something Jesus Christ capitalized on during His time on earth. To understand that, think for a moment about the word "Pharisee."

Contrary to what many believe, rank-and-file Pharisees were good people. In fact, they were great people, the kind you'd want as neighbors, serving on your city council, teaching in your schools, and building your roads and dams. They were true blue, believed in what was right, fair, honest, and godly—and worked like self-made, self-sustaining devils to do right by God and their fellow man (Romans 10:2).

But Camelot had a dark underbelly. Their leaders became experts at morphing the Mosaic Law (found in Exodus, Leviticus, Numbers, and Deuteronomy) into a complicated web of rules, rules about rules, and rules about rules subsumed under other rules.

At least three things resulted: First, the 'how to' manual perpetuated an oppressive leadership culture, insuring job security for the religious elite. "The people need us," they reasoned. "They're like sheep without a shepherd. We're the only ones who can decipher the Law's true meaning and teach them how to live so they make it into God's future perfect kingdom." Tragically, many people bought that lie and fed the monster with blind acclamation and respect. I'll leave it to you to find any example of that going well.

Second, those leaders made following God's Law—that is, being good enough to make it into God's kingdom—a debilitating mix of confusion and empty, dead ritual. God's heart, character, and the way He operates took a back seat to man-made (and thus doubt-filled) protocol designed to convince God somehow, some way, "We're good and noble enough to make it in on our own." Religion became man-centered, not God-centered. Knowing God—and being known by Him—wasn't much of a factor. Just doing what He said is what counted. People became prideful— or profoundly discouraged and spiritually-malnourished.

Third, as mentioned in chapter two, religious leaders cast the Mosaic Law as an achievable goal for winning His favor while ignoring the fact no human being is capable of reaching that level of perfection.

The apostle Paul knew the hypocrisy well. We've mentioned his peers thought he knew the rule book inside and out and was good at following it—prime among them, in fact (Galatians 1:14, Philippians 3:5-6). But his encounter with Jesus Christ on the road to Damascus caused a radical shift in his thinking (Acts 9:1-22). He realized all that work, all that zeal, all that "all for God and God alone" was destitute rubbish (Philippians 3:8). Human merit can never achieve God's approval because every life is riddled with sin. Here's how he put it to a fellow group of Pharisees:

> You therefore who teach another, do you not teach yourself? You who preach that one shall not steal, do you steal? You who say that one should not commit adultery, do you commit adultery? You who abhor idols, do you rob temples? You who boast in the Law, through your breaking the Law, do you dishonor God? For "THE

NAME OF GOD IS BLASPHEMED AMONG THE
GENTILES BECAUSE OF YOU," just as it is written.

ROMANS 2:21-24

Jesus Christ knew the hypocrisy, too. He told a group of Pharisees once, "Did not Moses give you the Law, and yet none of you carries out the Law?" (John 7:19). One has only to read Matthew 23:13-33 to understand how much their insincerity sickened Him. But it's important to understand *why.* He objected to self-righteousness (and the pride driving it) because it shifted the focus in the relationship to what we do for Him.

That was never God's intention. Ever. It was never His intention our relationship with Him be built on what we do. It's foundation is faith in what He did—and wants to do—for us. Even in the Old Testament, He couldn't have said it more clearly:

> Thus says the LORD, "Let not a wise man boast of his wisdom, and let not the mighty man boast of his might, let not a rich man boast of his riches; but let him who boasts boast of this, that he *understands and knows Me,* that I am the LORD who exercises lovingkindness, justice and righteousness on earth; for I delight in these things," declares the LORD.
>
> JEREMIAH 9:23-24 (emphasis mine)

> Blessed be the Lord, Who *daily* bears our burden, the God of our salvation.
>
> PSALM 68:19 (emphasis mine)

Many in the first century forgot the Old Testament taught Abraham was justified by faith, not works; and David didn't earn forgiveness for his adultery and murder (Genesis 15:1-6, 2 Samuel 12:13). In Jesus' day, Peter and Paul weren't required to do penance before the Lord commissioned them to serve Him (John 21:15-17, Acts 9:1-20). All they did was encounter and trust the God who proved He loved them by doing something for them they could never do on their own—pay the penalty for their sin and promise them life in heaven. Free of charge. Now and forever.

They also forgot Adam and Eve were perfect humans living in a perfect world with a perfect God—and they blew it. That means imperfect humans have *no chance* of living perfectly in an imperfect world. It's a truth everyone on the planet must face.

Doing so means realizing we need a shepherd. Bad. Not just any shepherd, clothed with humanity but nothing more. We need a Shepherd who is more than human, Someone with perfect knowledge and insight Who can winnow away the chaff of falsehood that chokes our spiritual lives to death. We need Someone to tell us what's really what and lead us home to heaven. We need God Himself to speak now and *not* forever hold His peace.

There He sat, in a boat a few feet off the shore of Lake Gennesaret, otherwise known as the Sea of Galilee (Luke 5:1-3). He spoke. The people listened. Intently.

When He finished, he told the boat's owner and his co-workers to put out in deep water and let their nets down for a catch. Simple enough, it would seem—but there was an objection.

"Master, we worked hard all night and caught nothing," the owner said (Luke 5:4-5a). It was his way of saying, "Rabbi, I'm not sure what your whole story is but we're fishermen. As in professional. Fishermen. We know, I say again, we *know* the best time to catch fish is in the middle of the night."

"It's why we were out there last night, doing everything we know to be successful, working hard to put bread on the table and a little security in the hearts of those we love. Otherwise, 'A little sleep, a little slumber, a little folding of the hands to sleep; so shall your poverty come on you like a prowler and your need like an armed man.'[3] Don't know if you're familiar with that or not. It's in the Bible … in uh … somewhere. Anyway, all we have to show for it are blistered hands and soiled nets. Now you're telling us to go out *again?*"

I don't know if it was the look on Jesus' face or if something else prompted the spokesman, Peter, to dispense with his objection. It doesn't matter. He did. He acted in faith, put out in the lake, and dropped his nets (Luke 5:5b).

The next thing he knew, he and his co-workers were wrestling a catch so large it was tearing their nets and sinking two of their boats (Luke 5:6-7). Unbelievable. All night, all for nothing. Then *He* shows up—and does for them what all their work and labor and sweat and toil and loss of sleep couldn't do.

Peter's response is interesting. Luke 5:8 tells us he rushed back to shore and "fell down at Jesus' feet, saying, 'Go away from me Lord, for I am a sinful man, O Lord!'" Peter didn't fully understand who was in front of Him—yet. But he knew somehow, God was there—and it made him immediately aware of his sin.

Yet please note. Before the miracle, Jesus did not require Peter to demonstrate his allegiance to God by reciting the Ten Commandments or show a letter of commendation from local religious leadership. He didn't ask him and his fellow fishermen to first make the roughly seventy-mile trek to Jerusalem to offer a sacrifice for their sins at the Temple.

He certainly could have. After all, whether they knew it or not, they were standing in the presence of God Himself. According to the Old Testament, only the High Priest could do that once a year on the Day of Atonement—and not before offering a sacrifice for his sins, bathing, putting on special garments to perform the necessary sacrifices for the entire nation, bathing again, and offering a burnt offering for himself and the people (Leviticus 16:3-4, 6, 24). Peter had dirt under his nails and smelled like fish. Yet that didn't hinder the Lord from doing for Peter and his friends what they couldn't do for themselves.

The culture demanded supreme dedication to rules and regulations before one could even *think* about God doing something for them. *Jesus Christ* required nothing but *helpless faith.* To drive the point home, observe what the Holy Spirit directed Luke to record next:

> While He was in one of the cities, behold, there was a man covered with leprosy; and when he saw Jesus, he fell on his face and implored Him, saying, "Lord, if You are willing, You can make me clean." And He stretched out His hand and touched him, saying, "I am willing; be cleansed." And immediately the leprosy left him.
>
> LUKE 5:12-13

Lepers were society's ultimate outcasts, forced to live away from civilization in colonies which kept their contagion at bay (Leviticus 13:46). Just as bad, they were ceremonially unclean, which meant they could not worship at the tabernacle (and later in history, at the Temple, Leviticus 13-14). There was no cure, other than a miraculous healing from God. Otherwise, the only thing a leper could do was beg for food and beg to die.

The leper who approached Jesus brought societal disdain, ceremonial shame, and a diseased body to the table. Nothing else. No merits, no grand list of accomplishments by which he enriched humanity. A polluted corpus before the pure Word of God. A good first century religious zealot wouldn't *think* about approaching a rabbi in that condition—much less, God Himself.

But Jesus wasn't looking for good first century zealots. He was looking for helpless people who had nothing but faith. No pedigree. No list of good works done. Nothing in any way, shape, or form which would convince anyone such a person had earned God's favor. Add to that the man was—like all men and women, boys and girls—a sinner, and who in their right mind would consider *that guy* a candidate for a miracle?

Jesus Christ, God in the flesh, would. He did. He touched him. The Perfect God purifying helpless, contaminated flesh. Beautiful.

Peter and his fishin' buddies were helpless. So was the leper, a man who could do nothing to remedy the condition of his body. (Remember that, by the way. It's an important theme in this book). Soon, a huge crowd would learn they were, too.

Chapter 7

SOME DISMANTLING
REQUIRED

Part Two

There He was, sitting again … this time before a large crowd on a mountain, just like Moses. That's not a coincidence. He was there to reveal the Mosaic Law's true depth and meaning, demonstrating He was not only taking Moses' place; He was Moses' God. Note also He was on a mountain in Galilee, the land of the Gentiles, fulfilling Isaiah's great prophecies that God's salvation is intended for the whole world (Isaiah 9:1-2, 19:18-25, 42:6-7, 49:6, 60:1-3).

Some hoped He was about to shipwreck what their leaders said Moses taught and the prophets affirmed. They couldn't wait. The dead orthodoxy of the religious elite needed to be buried once and for all. They'd labored under its requirements, trying harder yet always losing ground, and were tired of it. Dog tired. The funeral couldn't happen fast enough.

Others were raising their eyebrows, having heard rumors this new rabbi brought an entirely new teaching, completely counter-cultural to the status quo. It's what youth does, tossing aside 'the way we've always done it' to make a name for itself. "Do not think I came to abolish the Law or the Prophets," He told them. "I did not come to abolish but to fulfill" (Matthew 5:17).

"Great," the hopeful funeral-goers must have thought. "The same old stuff. To think I hauled my entire family up here to hear everything I'd hoped we wouldn't. More burdens. More rules. More 'thou shalt nots' wrapped in 'there's no way thou cans.' Great. Super. Can't wait to hear this."

The rule makers, self-proclaimed guardians of everything holy and orthodox, likely breathed a sigh of relief. "Well, alrighty then. Maybe the new kid's not so bad. Sounds like he's one of us. Let's hear him out."

It was the perfect set up for what Jesus Christ said next, something neither side could have imagined. "For I say to you unless your righteousness surpasses that of the scribes and Pharisees, you will not enter the kingdom of heaven" (Matthew 5:20).

"I'm sorry … what was that? Did … did he just murder Moses? Did He just say even the *experts* don't have a chance of making it?" Sorry to rain on your parade but yes, that's exactly what He said.

He kept going. In verses 21-47, Jesus Christ made clear Law-saturated notions of obedience were soaked in delusion. For instance, from God's perspective, avoiding murder isn't enough; one has to prove he never called anyone a mildly derogatory name. To do so is to set yourself up as judge and jury, assaulting God and someone created in His image. You might as well tell the Almighty *He's* the idiot. Do that once and there is hell to pay, literally (Matthew 5:22).

Forgiveness is equally demanding (5:23-26). Left on our own, every time we offend or hurt someone, His standard demands we go to them immediately and seek forgiveness. To forget it, blow it off, rationalize it as 'no big deal' or assume 'she'll get over it' is not an option.

Adultery is no different (Matthew 5:27-30). Avoiding the act isn't good enough—not for a God who sees thought and action with the same high-definition clarity. If we attempt to argue since we never did the deed we're innocent, at Judgment Day He'll peel open every nook and cranny of every thought we ever had and expose every lustful impulse, no matter how brief. All we'll hear is "Guilty!"

Divorce? Unless it's for reasons He allows it's a 'no go' (Matthew 5:31-32).[4] Make a rash vow, fail to fulfill a promise, or swear we're telling the truth when there's a little white lie lurking? God is not like that. We are—which means we're evil—and evil people can't live in heaven (Psalm 5:4, Matthew 5:33-37).

How about revenge—an eye for an eye and all that? Have we ever taken matters in our own hands rather than let God handle it in His time, His way—even if it means waiting until Judgment Day? Sorry. That's a one-and-done (Matthew 5:38-42).

How about loving only those who love us? Is God like that? He gives good things to evil people (Luke 6:35). Do we? Do we pray for people who have it in for us—or is grace and mercy only dispensed to those who, in our judgment, have earned it (Matthew 5:43-47)?

"Therefore," He concluded, "you are to be perfect, as your heavenly Father is perfect" (5:48).

Suddenly, it didn't matter if you were regular folk seeking rules relief, a well-intentioned, sincere adherent trying your best to make it to heaven, or a double-minded leader doing it all for show. It didn't matter. No one was safe. No one could meet the

---

4. Permissible reasons are sexual immorality (Matthew 5:31-32, 19:3-9) and desertion by an unbelieving spouse (1 Corinthians 7:10-15).

standard. Even if one dared argue he or she was totally sinless in one area, we're not in *every* area and that makes us guilty of the entire Law (James 2:10-11, Galatians 5:1-3). As we've learned, God is One which means His Law and standards are, too. Righteousness isn't divided up piecemeal. Neither is guilt.

Never One to do things halfway, Jesus didn't let up. In Matthew 6 and 7, He took a sledgehammer to first century notions of charitable giving, prayer, fasting for show, materialism, anxiety, judging others, wisdom, relationships—all of it was on the chopping block, replaced by a standard so exact and unforgiving it was as foreign as a gearbox on an oxcart.

He finished with this: If they didn't listen to Him, didn't live up to the standards He shared, it would be like building a house on a sandbar. Disaster (temporal and eternal) would eventually strike, no exceptions. Everything they had, treasured, and hoped for would be swept away (7:24-27).

Most translations say the crowd was "amazed at His teaching" (7:28). But the sense of the word in context is they were "stirred up, unsettled or astonished" (see Matthew 19:25 for an example). Their mouths dropped open. They looked at each other with the sinking feeling that comes when we get *that* call or hear *that* news. Hope evaporated. Completely.

God had given God's perspective. There would be no petitioning Him for an amendment. As we've said before, He does not stutter. He never second-guesses Himself. He does not use grand-sounding ambiguities to veil clarity. All Truth is His Truth and His Truth is The Truth. Always. No exceptions.

God had just *clearly* said self-righteousness, self-justification, self-forgiveness, and self-generated-and-focused worth are the biggest illusions in human history. Like the Ten Commandments, the Sermon on the Mount was a declaration on how to live, yes—but it was also a mirror on the human soul inscribed with a death sentence. All those people clamoring for words of life and hope found exactly the opposite. They weren't emboldened, emancipated, or good to go. They were enlightened sheep for the slaughter on a slow boat to hell.

Unless they could find a Savior—Someone equal to the task of meeting God's standards of perfection and somehow, in some way, gracious enough to share the benefit with them, they had no chance. But who can meet God's standards but God Himself? And who can cover sin against God but God Himself?

They were right where He wanted them.

If you were that Savior—and wanted to reassure a stunned crowd condemning words of exacting perfection were, in fact, an invitation to enjoy something You could do for them they could never do for themselves—what would You do right after delivering that message?

> When Jesus came down from the mountain, large crowds followed Him. And a leper came to Him and bowed down before Him, and said, "Lord, if You are willing, You can make me clean." Jesus stretched out His hand and touched him, saying, "I am willing; be cleansed." And immediately his leprosy was cleansed.
>
> MATTHEW 8:1-3

If that sounds remarkably like Luke's account of the leper in Luke 5, it should (see chapter six). The point is precisely the same:

All that religion, all that rigor, all those rules, all that effort born of education or expertise, all that self-induced stuff we think makes us look good to others but does nothing to cure the sin lurking where the world can't see it—should be thrown in the garbage. In essence, Jesus Christ was showing the world He didn't come to show us what we must do for God. He came first and foremost to show us what God wants to do for people whose souls are rancid with sin and can't do anything about it.

To accomplish that mission, He had to completely dismantle first century Judaism. It was too twisted, too tied up in works instead of faith. It replaced God's desire to radically alter imperfect men with His grace with the conviction we didn't need Him—or His mercy, really. *Our effort* could lift us to a level of righteousness commensurate with His and persuade Him to give us the keys to His kingdom. The Old Testament Law, centered in the Ten Commandments, became the roadmap to perfection instead of a tutor to show us our sin and lead us to salvation in Christ (John 5:39-40, Galatians 3:24).

That may seem like Christianity 101. But to those entombed in the collective peer pressure of centuries-long tradition, it was anything but. To drive the point home, one day in Jerusalem the Lord stood before the Temple and offered a prediction which shook the powers-that-be right down to the base of their Western wall.

> And while some were talking about the temple, that it was adorned with beautiful stones and votive gifts, He said, "As for these things which you are looking at, the days will come in which there will not be left one stone upon another which will not be torn down."
>
> LUKE 21:5-6

For centuries, the Temple represented God's presence among His people. But self-proclaimed religious experts had chiseled it into a gravestone of dead orthodoxy. Greed drove money-hungry merchants in its outer courts to sell animals for sacrifice at exorbitant prices. The wealthy, more interested in showing off than showing humility, paraded by Temple coffers adorned with large, trumpet-like funnels which made all kinds of racket when coins were tossed in. The louder the noise, the more heads turned in admiration of such glorious benevolence. Like everything else in their brand of religion, pride ransacked virtue.

It was time for the grand symbol of religious life, the one fathers boldly pointed out to their children as the great logo of God's pleasure and blessing, to come tumbling down. Pride goes before destruction, as the Proverb says (16:18). When the Romans demolished Jerusalem in A.D. 70 and destroyed the Temple, that literally came true.

It was the ultimate irony. The God of the universe standing in bodily form in front of an empty edifice He once called home. The Temple of God face-to-face with *a* temple of God. The Body and Blood about to dismantle the place where the bodies and blood of animals temporarily accomplished what He was about to set in a stone to be rolled from the tomb. It had served its purpose. It was time for the building to go and the Temple to remain, to dismantle one body which, no matter how glamorous or well-kept, was still beset with sin and imperfection—and replace it with another.

He does that with other bodies, too.

Chapter 8

MAY I HAVE YOUR TENSION ... PLEASE?

I don't ride roller coasters anymore because the last time I did, I passed out. Too bad, too. Despite a bout of nausea now and then, I loved a good loop de loop as much as anyone. But intestinal bungee jumps now coupled with a loss of connection to the space-time continuum made me realize "a snow cone and that bench over there" is a better alternative. I guess I really have become my parents.

It strikes me when souls such as I (was) prefer pulling G's to amusement park benches, a curious phenomenon occurs just before it all breaks loose. As riders take their seats in cars destined to speed them to the edge of death, substantial bars and/or cage-like structures lock them in place. It's as if the ride designers are standing there saying, "If you want a full body experience, you need a body in lockdown."

In my years among the intrepid, I don't recall objections to the paradox. On the contrary, enthusiasts embrace the notion the end-game—loops, corkscrews, hairpin turns, stomach churning drops—and the laughter and stories that go with them—is only achieved by restriction to sitting, holding on, and putting their hands in the air. The ability to run, jump, dance, spin, catch a ball, drive a car, cook dinner, and hug a loved one are all gone. "Not here, ladies and gentlemen. You want the payoff, you accept the restriction."

"No problem," friends and family say to each other. "Just wait 'til that howitzer of a launch system rifles us outta here. We won't give a rip about 'restrictions'!"

What is true of roller coasters is also true of the resurrection. Before you and I discover the thrill of racing from old age to youth in the ten milliseconds it takes to get to heaven, our bodies must be locked down and limited. Drooling, incoherent thoughts pooling at the base of a sentence have not given way to endless waves of effortless wisdom or talent and athleticism that would be the envy of every Grammy-winner or gold-medalist in this age. Our present reality is the creeping limitations of now and the limitlessness of then are bunkmates.

It's quite a paradox.

And it isn't easy, is it?

———— ❧ ————

I couldn't believe it. What did I just do?

Like countless times before, I reached into the refrigerator for milk to pour over my cereal. Cap off, grasp handle. Lift and dispense. No problem. Could do this in my sleep. Replace cap, hoist, and put back in the...

Food pantry?

Where canned beans and chips live? Where oatmeal and pop-corn trade stories of the good ol' days at the store talking to mixed nuts and nicknaming swing-shift stockers? Where beans and rice swap recipes; and soft drinks on the floor daydream of a better view from the third shelf? Where the only thing below thirty seven degrees that goes near the place is a family member's hand after putting ice cream back in the freezer ...?

That's where I put the milk?

There's a perfectly justifiable reason, of course. The pantry door is just to the right of the refrigerator door. One is metallic silver with a curved handle long enough to travel from my ankle to my waist. The other is white with a brushed-nickel door knob the size of a small ramekin. Easy mistake. Everyone knows this.

Yet I know better. The neural processes in my younger self would have made the fine distinctions between size, shape, com-position, and location of the appropriate door and, without error or hesitation, aided by hundreds of thousands of highly-coor-dinated, athletically-charged motor responses, placed said milk in the proper place—all the while occupying it's nimble, youth-laden spare brain power with a replay of last night's game and a recitation of the Gettysburg address to keep from, well, los-ing its mind from boredom. My older, present-self said, "Door. Dere. Dat works."

I wish it had only happened once. Once is humorous. If I'd been in high school, my friends would have erupted with laugh-ter and nicknamed me "Milkman." But these days, every day, I do something like that. I recently defrosted salmon in cold water and put it in the silver-handled *microwave* to chill for dinner. When it was time to cook, it took me and my wife, Dawn, five minutes to find it. I know what I was thinking—and that's what scares me. "Appliance. Silver handle. Gotta be it."

I knew I would get old. I just can't believe it's actually happening. It's humbling. Truth be told, I don't care for it much. I can't plead I had a "junior moment" like I could twenty years ago. It's become a commentary, a proclamation of the new normal, a prediction of things to come. The network is slowly shutting down and there's not a whole lot I can do about it. I eat right. I exercise. I build new neural pathways with a hobby that demands I do things I'm not used to doing. But the clock is ticking. Like it or not, age twenty is so far behind me I can't tell if it's still there or just a speck of wishful dust on life's rearview mirror. Ditto for a number of other decade-marking birthdays.

I'm degrading.

We all are.

The same effort yields things done half as fast in twice the time. "Less is more" has become "more is less." When did *that* happen? I still *feel* the same. I'm still convinced I can do anything I set out to do. Mind over matter, right?

Years ago, I worked for a well-known author whose oldest son was about to get married. His groomsmen decided pre-ceremony festivities should include a game of pick-up basketball. The older guys on my boss' staff (including me) were invited to join in.

Naturally, the gathering turned into geezers vs. the young guns. No problem. Me and my older, more experienced, finely-tuned athletic comrades thought, "Pfffff. No problem. Like taking candy from a baby. We'll wax these rookies with one hand tied behind our backs."

About five minutes into the game, the guy I guarded dribbled in from half-court. I was on him like a duck on a June bug. A few seconds later, the look on his face, where his eyes went, and the way he side-palmed the ball telegraphed he was about to attempt a pass between my legs. A sly smile crept across the face of my inner NBA legend. "In your dreams, dude. Not happenin.' You need a better chance to have no chance."

He started the pass and I shuttered my legs like a performance-enhanced Venus flytrap. I mean, it was greased lightnin' ridin' side car on the speed of light. Yet before I could mumble "James Naismith," the ball blew past my axial—appendicular junction and landed squarely in his teammate's hands. Stunned, I looked down, sure I'd moved every bit of real estate in the lower forty eight to block that pass. The reality was a few muscles had twitched with barely-discernible spasms of intention and my right knee was bent inward about ten degrees.

I was thirty.

It was my first introduction to the years ahead, ones which slowly, painfully tutor all of us that intention and results are no longer the same. As the years churn by, we realize purveyors of "you can achieve whatever you put your mind too" are preachers of a false gospel imparted to the young because they're still idealistic and inexperienced enough to believe it. As days become decades, we learn that's not always true. We see youth for what it is, a momentary pitstop on the way to something far more long-lasting: diminished abilities and dissipated dreams.

Sure, hopeful words of a bright, eternal future are fine—until nerve-endings are on fire, needles prod, and walking requires we look up to see straight ahead. It doesn't take much to add our voice to the psalmist who said ...

> Our heart has not turned back, and our steps have not deviated from Your way. Yet You have crushed us in a place of jackals, and covered us with the shadow of death.
>
> PSALM 44:18-19

The world's story-tellers end the tale right there. They believe all we see is all there is and will be, that the world is an amalgam of materialistically reductionist processes ending in nothingness, nothing more. They forget the things which drive and shape the human experience—as powerful as gravity and black holes—have no mass or physical mechanism and yet are just as real: love, loyalty, compassion, grace, forgiveness, and eternal life; hate, betrayal, jealousy, envy, and strife. They ignore that the human spirit yearns for the triumph of the former over the latter (as witnessed in countless good vs. evil stories—not to mention stories of resurrection) and fail to ask why.

Why? It's because there's something embedded in us, something we cannot shake, that this existence can't be all there is. Something better looms. It must. It's echoed in every corner of the globe, from eastern religion's Nirvana to American pop culture's belief when someone dies "They're in a better place."

The only explanation is those ideals, call them the grand pillars of human existence, were there from the beginning. That means they are eternal—and we believe in them because we have a deep sense *we* are eternal. Which means there's more to the story when we're no longer above ground (Ecclesiastes 3:11).

It also means living with the God-ordained strain of knowing we aren't there yet, which means we're not as good as we could be. The better person we hope to be isn't the one looking at us in the mirror. We know we should be a more consistent manifestation of the fruit of the Spirit (Galatians 5:22-23). Yet too often we judge the 55-year-old flipping burgers for not being ambitious enough, fire off the vengeful comeback which decimates someone made in God's image, or look the other way when we see tears streaming down the face of someone sitting alone in the airport. Yes, the Lord views us as if we've never sinned, in fact, as if we can't sin.

But His viewpoint and our experience aren't One yet. We live in the now and He sees us from then—and the gap is enormous.

That means until He steps in and makes all things new again, Jesus Christ calls us to live in the tension of *the now and the not-yet*—trusting Him for the strength to press failing arms and legs against the parallel walls of hope and despair, inching our way up and out of this life into the next. And since body, soul, and spirit are one just as He is, it means living with our eyes glued to His portrait of us, the present one He sees from the future (i.e. our perfection) while we struggle to slap away the hands of an enemy pressing our face into the mirror of sin-pillaged disfigurement.

Satan's mission is to convince us the pain of that disfigurement is the legacy of having lived. We can barely walk. It's hard to follow a movie's plot line. Skills honed through decades of employment atrophy by the month and we grieve their loss. Our schedule, once full of things which gave us meaning and purpose, is now constipated with doctor's visits and lab appointments. People don't need us, we're forgotten at work, and death is beginning to take people we love. The tug-of-war between what we want to believe and what we see and experience is too much. The tension is too much. Add to that God orchestrates all of it (Job 5:17-18, Isaiah 45:7, Lamentations 3:38)—and thus doesn't care about us—and its game over.

Jesus Christ is asking us to let Him have every bit of that tension ... please. He knows we live with a daily restlessness for the redemption of all things (Romans 8:20-23) and are tempted to believe Satan's narrative is true. Still, He wants us to wait, to accept imperfection, restriction, and limitation as tools He's using to strip away the adversary's caricatures and misdirections of reality.

As counterintuitive as it seems, He wants us to believe He's powerful enough to use the tension and imperfection of *now* to cut off the enemy's hands (which feed us lies) and replace them with His own. Indeed, we are inscribed on His palms (Isaiah 49:15-16, a metaphorical prophecy of the loving benefits of His crucifixion) and His righteous Right Hand is there to strengthen, help, and uphold us when fear and anxiousness strike (Isaiah 41:10). It means trusting He's using the lull between now and then to craft the perfect from the imperfect, preparing us for the moment when heaven takes hold.

Make no mistake. *That* is an act of faith. But as with all things in life, Jesus never asks us to walk a path He hasn't. It's why He was willing to "be made like His brethren in all things" (Hebrews 2:17). He left the glory of heaven, lived in a human body with "no stately form or majesty that we should look upon Him, nor appearance that we should be attracted to Him" (Isaiah 53:2, Philippians 2:6-8), and faced temptation, pain, and suffering to the highest degree possible (Hebrews 4:14-16). He knows what it is to agonize while waiting for deliverance, to suffer in a body that doesn't work anymore, to carry the load of promises not yet fulfilled—and how to help those enduring that burden right now (Matthew 26:37-44, Hebrews 2:14-18, 5:7-9).

He also knows it's worth it (John 17:5, Philippians 2:9-11, Hebrews 12:1-3).

In our twenties and thirties, we know death will come. But it's like a 200-foot-wall on the horizon, ten miles away. It's easy to give it a quick glance then gaze elsewhere because other things consume our field of vision. In our fifties, the wall is closer—and larger. We know a few who've climbed it; we must look harder not to see it. Ditto for our sixties.

Grow much older and The Wall looms as the dominant structure on the landscape. It's everywhere, as far as the eye can see. Gray, menacing, and lifeless, it drones a grim, dissonant funeral chant. Retirement, then death. Isn't that how the script reads?

Just exactly how do you feel about that?

Chapter 9

WHO'S AT MIDFIELD?

One day, a person we've likely never met will place still, lifeless hands to our side—ones which can no longer write a bucket list or reach for the brass ring—and close the coffin on desires unfulfilled, tasks undone, and experiences untried. The exuberance of youth, ours for a moment and vainly pursued for a lifetime, will surrender to silhouettes of skin and bone lying motionless on the edge of eternity. Day is done. Gone the sun.

If we chafe at that, good. We should. There's something wrong and unnatural about a life brought into existence by an eternal God only to see Him superintend its demise. How can an eternal, depthless God, the great "One," create anything not destined for eternal re-creation, redemption, or resolution?

As we discovered in chapter one, with the exception of the demonic realm, the answer is, "He can't." God cannot and will not walk out of the stadium of this age with sin holding the trophy at midfield. Jesus Christ proved that beyond a shadow of a doubt when the Holy Spirit's power exploded His body from the grave, demonstrating the agony of sin—and its ultimate expression, death—could not hold Him in its grip (Acts 2:24). The same Spirit, with the same power, dwells in every Christian. He inspired Paul to put it this way:

> But if the Spirit of Him who raised Jesus from the dead dwells in you, He who raised Christ Jesus from the dead will also give life to your mortal bodies through His Spirit who dwells in you.
>
> Romans 8:11

Giving life to our mortal bodies isn't just a metaphorical way of saying He'll help us live faithfully here. That's true but there's more to it. Life continues after death. That's why it's called *eternal* life. He has commissioned our journey to be like Him, culminating in the same expulsion from the grave He experienced. He was raised from the dead; we will be raised from the dead—with imperishable bodies marked by glory and power, just like His (1 Corinthians 6:14, 15:42-43). The One Who began a good work in us at the moment of faith will successfully bring all aspects of it to completion (Philippians 1:6).

As we discussed in chapter eight, right now we're enduring the trial-laden part of the journey, following the same path He did when He was here. No, He never had a hip replaced or knew the embarrassment of chronic incontinence. But He did know the rejection and abandonment of those He loved, the hatred of enemies, and what it was like to have His bones slip out of their sockets while He hung in agony, barely clothed, for a mocking world to see. Yet He was willing to suffer all that because He knew the eternal payoff was far greater than the temporary pain.

Too often, the agonizing *now* of our journey blinds us to the same payoff. We need to remember that while affirming our trib-ulation here, the Lord told us to be of good cheer because He has overcome the world (John 16:33). It's a promise of something greater and far more real, one He wants us to cling to as we trace His footsteps, mimicking His endurance while He waited for the joy on the other side of His suffering (Hebrews 12:2).

The day is coming when there will be no more crying, disease, pain, death, or imperfection (Revelation 21:4). No more *age* and the atrocities it commits against the image of God we imperfectly bear. Day is done. Here comes the Son—to perfectly redeem the way He made us by re-installing our physical perfection, gifts, and abilities. It starts when we leave here and go home to heaven. It will continue when we return to this world, fully equipped to serve and reign with Him, and involve many things I'm sure we can't imagine (Daniel 7:13-18). But it's not hard to believe it will also involve the redemption of the "I wish I had" list in chapter five, which means …

Our love of learning, carpentry, engineering, piano, flying, invention, art, philanthropy, flowers, children, ballet, ministry, technology, the natural world, writing, song writing, sports, soft-ware, cooking, medicine, teaching, jewelry, project management, coaching, law and justice, photography, defending dignity and freedom, animals, dentistry, ranching, construction, architecture—all of it will be adapted to a world where He reigns supreme and commissions us to use our Spirit-enabled aptitudes to serve Him—completely bereft of hassle, heartache, disappointment, physical limitation, or flaw.

You will cook a soufflé as only you can. You will whisper and horses will hear. Your lips on brass or woodwinds; or fingers on strings or keys will paint images of His beauty on the hearts of men and angels—in a way completely unique to you. The building you construct will display His glory and your fingerprint. All of it will be a celebration of Who He Is and His partnership with us. Concerns over a paycheck or what our parents wanted us to do for a living will be a thing of the past.

The days of mind over body as the path to accomplishment will be over, too. What our Spirit-directed minds want to do, our Spirit-energized bodies will happily oblige. Imagine needing to be shown how to do something only once—or instantly knowing how because of the fully-matured rows of instinct He's planted in us. Adam and Eve, you've got company.

There is a present-day hint of all this in at least three passages. First, Genesis 11:1-9 shows mankind, while bearing the effects of sin, still carried the residual effects of Garden of Eden prowess. We decided to build a tower to heaven so we could, apparently, ascend to God's position and mutiny.

In a remarkable statement, "The Lord said, 'Behold they are one people; and they all have the same language. And this is what they began to do, and now *nothing which they purpose to do will be impossible for them*'" (v. 6, emphasis mine). To prevent the fullest expression of man ennobled by sin, God wisely confused our language and supernaturally scattered us across the globe (vv. 7-8). But the point remains we were originally created to do anything we could conceive of. It makes sense God has every intention of restoring that ability in the future.

Second, Psalm 37 pictures our ability to collaborate with God in a way few of us can imagine. Verse 3 instructs us to "Trust in the Lord and do good; dwell in the land and cultivate faithfulness" which sets up what follows: "Delight yourself in the Lord; and He will give you the desires of your heart. Commit your way to the Lord, trust also in Him and He will do it" (verses 4-5).

The Hebrew word "commit" means "to roll" or "roll away." In

this context, the sense is to "roll" or "unfurl" our plans before the Lord. It pictures us as an architect unrolling a blueprint He enthusiastically endorses, along with a commitment to partner with us so it comes to pass. It's a beautiful picture of the collaboration He had with us once and jealously wants again.

We see an example in Adam naming the animal kingdom (Genesis 2:19). God's part was to bring every living creature to him. Adam's part was to name them—and he had free reign, i.e. "*Whatever* the man called a living creature, that was its name (emphasis mine)." Adam's intellectual and creative prowess aside, note there's no indication God ever corrected him. He never said, "Boy, I don't know, A… I'm not sure 'orangutan' is gonna work. People will forever mispronounce it 'oraguhtang.' Let's try something else." The theme of the moment was, "Adam, whatever you want is fine with Me."

"Elephant."

"I can hear its trumpet now."

"Eagle."

"That soars."

"Gorilla."

"Love it. Your kids will go ape for that."

"I'm sorry, Lord… kids?"

"I'll explain later."

"Horse."

"Well, hay. A horse is a horse of course, of course…"

"Canary."

"Man, that sings."

"Wolf."

"No dog in my book."

"Thanks, Lord. This is fun. Hey, by the way. I've been working on some poetry. Tell me what You think of this…"

Oh, there once a platypus named Chuck,
Who borrowed the bill of a duck.
He stumbled and fell,
And as you can tell,
The bill to his face became stuck.

I'll leave it to you to imagine the look on the Lord's face. That experience isn't ours yet—at least not totally. Yes, ministries and great projects come to pass because a human vision fit a divine plan. But in this age, everything we come up with is subject to God's refinement, redirection, temporary suspension, or cancellation. As most can attest, for every success, there are a hundred ideas which fall by the wayside. Sin, a plan we think is great but isn't, our inability to execute it, or it's misalignment with His will (which we may never understand here) are all factors. It's why Proverbs 16:9 is important to remember: "The mind of man plans his way, but the Lord directs His steps."

Yet that won't always be the case. One day, when He's redeemed our bodies, minds, hearts, and souls in an amalgam of unity and perfection we can't begin to describe, Proverbs 16:9 will be a museum piece. There will be no disconnect between what we come up with and what He wants. We will be, as the Lord prayed, one, as He and the Father are One, perfected in unity with Him and each other (John 17:11, 20-23).

Our plans will be His plans, without blemish, error, or misunderstanding. We will know the full experience of abiding in Him (and His Word in us) so He grants whatever we ask (John 15:7). He will never say, "No." Ever.[5]

---

5. For another example of collaboration with God, see David's interaction with Him in 1 Chronicles 28 regarding construction of the Temple. In vv. 11-12, David shares with Solomon the plans "he [David] had in mind." In v. 19, he says "All this [that is, plans for the Temple] … the Lord made me understand in writing by His hand upon me, all the details of this pattern."

The third passage is Luke 12:32. In encouraging His listeners to stop worrying about their needs because God the Father would meet them, Jesus Christ said: "Do not be afraid, little flock, for Your Father has *gladly chosen* to give you the kingdom" (emphasis mine). That is, we will be the beneficiaries of all the rights and privileges perfect humans deserve to enjoy in a kingdom prepared for *us* since the foundation of the world (Matthew 25:34). Just as Adam and Eve were commissioned to imitate Him as they superintended creation, God will recommission us to do the same when He makes a new heaven and earth in which righteousness dwells (2 Peter 3:13).

All things.

In all ways.

Summed up, redeemed, and made perfect in Him.

None of this is to say God is our ultimate genie, obligated to fulfill earthly dreams and desires simply because we had them. "The heart is more deceitful than all else and is desperately sick; who can understand it?" (Jeremiah 17:9). The answer is "God can" (1 Kings 8:39, 1 Chronicles 28:9, Psalm 33:15). He knows our make up with indescribable precision. He knows what we think we want, how we think we're made, or what we think we're good at isn't necessarily the case. He knows the skills, abilities, and aptitudes that are dormant or underdeveloped in us because He put them there—and He understands precisely how and when to bring them out.

In this world, we may have fancied ourselves a drummer or dressmaker. We may have even done it for a living. But He knows something else will give us even more satisfaction, more joy, and more pleasure in enjoying how He made us—so much so that when He ignites it in us in the future, we could easily find ourselves saying, "Drumming? Dress-making? What in the world was I thinking?" Indeed, one of the great joys of eternity may be the realization He *prevented what we hoped to do here to set us up for what we hope for there.* He's the only One in the universe who knows the difference. Whatever the details, our sentiment will be what Scottish runner, Olympic champion, and missionary, Eric Liddell once told his sister, Jenny: "God made me fast. And when I run, I feel His pleasure."[6]

It's also important to remember everything we experience here is preparation for what awaits. In Hebrews 2:5-8, the Holy Spirit quotes Psalm 8:4-6 to shed light on our future life in Christ's kingdom. Then in 2:10, He speaks of "bringing many sons to glory" meaning He takes us through our paces in this life (including hardship) to fully equip us for our role in the next. As one commentator says,

> At present God is not saving the human race entire and its affairs corporate, but is selecting from it the company that are to rule the universe, superseding the existing government. He is preparing for a complete reorganization of His entire empire, and is giving to these future rulers the severe training which is indispensable to fitting them for such responsible duties and high dignities… There is manifest wisdom in a great Leader first training a body of efficient subordinates before seeking to reorganize society at large.[7]

6. https://www.goodreads.com/author/quotes/802465.Eric_Liddell
7. G.H. Lang quoted in "The Epistle to the Hebrews" class notes by Zane Hodges, Professor of New Testament, Dallas Theological Seminary, Spring Semester, 1984, p. 70.

None of this is to say the future will be "us centered." The future is His. It is about Him. It should be. No greater Love, no greater Grace, no greater Person exists. To be with Him, in His universe His way, is to be positioned "so that in the ages to come He might show the surpassing riches of His grace in kindness toward us in Christ Jesus" (Ephesians 2:7). Only He could conceive of and execute an existence bearing eternal expressions of that Grace and Kindness.

It will be the best of all possible worlds, superintended, held together, and perpetually driven by The One relentlessly committed to shepherding us through "momentary, light affliction" here for the payoff of "an eternal weight of glory far beyond all comparison" (2 Corinthians 4:17; see Romans 8:18 also). In the ages to come, in all ways and at all times, He will be the center of attention. We, in all ways and at all times, will be the central focus of His Love.

Yet an important question lingers: How does the decline of our bodies prepare us for that? How do ailments like arthritis, heart disease, cancer, and dementia signal we're not getting old … we're getting ready?

Chapter 10

WE'RE GETTING READY

Part One

Boot camp.

Oh, what sweet serenity.

Yelling for breakfast. Shouting for lunch. Chaos for dinner. Shine this, polish that. I can't hear you! Drop and give me twenty. Rucksacks, rifles, and ten mile marches, fully loaded. There's a thread hanging off the third button down on your dress blues. Extra PT for you. The floor isn't clean enough. Clean it again. With a toothbrush.

Is all that really necessary? After all, when your platoon is eating dust and dodging bullets and bombs, does it really matter if your boots are dirty and your shirttail is hanging out?

Ask your drill instructor and you'll likely be told to hold your rifle over your head until you're told to put it down. That's because drill instructors know recruits must let go of every form of conventional thinking and doing to become what they've never been. Or, to paraphrase a famous quote from martyred missionary Jim Elliot, men and women in the military must lose what they cannot keep to gain what they cannot lose. It's true of athletic, musical, or academic training—and it's true of the Christian life, too. More to the point, it's true of the bodies we inhabit. There is rigor and hardship in giving up the body we cannot keep to gain the one we cannot lose.

It's tempting to think putting us through all that difficulty is the most ungodly thing God could do. After all, if He sees us as perfect, why make us live and die like we aren't? Why can't He just sustain us here as twenty-five-year-olds then instantly haul us to heaven when our three score and ten are done (Psalm 90:10)?

Truthfully, He could. He is the God of all flesh; nothing is too difficult for Him (Jeremiah 32:27). That He doesn't means He has a Deep Six reason not to, i.e. His compassion, grace, patience, loyal love, truth, and justice are driving the situation. There is no other explanation. He cannot countermand His moral makeup.

Those virtues even apply to what may seem the most counter-cultural truth in the Bible, one we encountered in chapter two: "The Lord has made everything for its own purpose, even the wicked for the day of evil" (Proverbs 16:4). That means He has a good purpose in allowing sin—and its adjutant generals aging and death—free access to humanity; and rather than mangle the Deep Six, they accelerate them.

Satan does not want us to believe that. He'll flex every lying muscle he has to convince us there is *no way* God is powerful enough to use sin to accomplish its polar opposite. According to his script, God is worried sick about how to solve a problem He allowed in and has no idea how to solve.

Which means Satan's assault on Job to teach him the vanity of self-righteousness and the need for humility, Pharoah's deceptive dealings with Israel to display God's power, His people's errant request for a king to teach them God was to be their king, David's

sinful census as a means to secure the Temple mount in Jerusalem, king Rehoboam's lack of wisdom which led to the fulfill-
ment of God's promise to Jeroboam, the prophet Hosea's fidelity
to an adulterous wife to illustrate God's love for His people, His
use of an evil nation to discipline His people for their sin, Jesus'
deliberate choice of an embezzler and traitor (Judas Iscariot) and
prideful religious elites to put Him to death to accomplish our
salvation, and Paul and Barnabas' disagreement over Mark's role
in missionary work as a means to extend the gospel's reach (Job
1-3, Exodus 9:16, 1 Samuel 8:1-22, 1 Kings 11:29-31 and 1 Kings
12:1-15, 1 Chronicles 21, Hosea 1-3, Habakkuk 1:5-11, John 6:70-
71, 11:53, 12:4-6, 13:27-30, Acts 15:36-40) … God had no hand
in any of that. It was just a bit of cosmic serendipity.

We're free to believe that lie if we want. Or we can choose the
biblical option that God wraps His hand in every lightning bolt,
commanding each to strike the mark;[8] controls the birth of every
animal across the globe; oversees every roll of every dice everywhere, all the time; guides countless galaxies, stars, planets, qua-
sars, pulsars, and black holes through the heavens, calling each
by name; controls when every bird on earth falls to the ground;
and at any moment we might ask, can tell us the exact number of
hairs on our head (Job 36:32, 38:35, 39:1-4, Psalm 147:4, Proverbs 16:33, Isaiah 40:25-26, Matthew 10:29-30).

That gets my vote—which means Satan is exactly who Jesus
Christ said he is: a liar and murderer in whom there is no truth.
For all the static, pain, and disruption he's causing, all he's really
doing is flailing around on the burning ash heap of history until
he and his angels become glowing embers of eternal punishment
(Matthew 8:29, 25:41, John 8:44, Revelation 20:10).

---

8. Scientists tell us lightning strikes the earth one hundred times per second. That does not count
cloud-to-cloud strikes or other forms of lightning like elves, sprites, and blue jets.

Until then, Jesus Christ calls us to ignore Satan's lies and finger-pointing and look past the shadows of death and old age. With our focus on the future, we fulfill the purpose of waning youth here, confident it's not the enemy's gavel but a mallet wielded by the Ultimate Sculptor, chiseling perfection from fragility.

It's tempting to think between now and then all we can do is watch chunks of ourselves fall to the ground as the Sculptor does His work. With each painful strike, there is less of us. What was once strong, vibrant, and capable is no longer. There is less to offer others and less for them to love. We fear they will cringe at the sights, sounds, and odor of our dismantling.

Yet eyes of faith, with vision sharpened by years of trusting Him, enable us to see faltering bodies create a perfect partnership with Him to display what the apostle Paul came to understand: While we always carry around the dying of Jesus in our bodies, we do so to ultimately manifest His power in the resurrection (2 Corinthians 4:10).

That's daunting, I know. But take heart. He has no intention of letting us shoulder the burden alone. He knows—and we can trust—that while difficult mental, emotional, and physical offloading is required to prepare us for the incredible place we're headed, He's with us every step of the way, completing work in and through us so we're ready for the moment death fades to Life. Like a good auto mechanic, He knows what He's doing, can be trusted to do His work well, and has not taken us for a ride on the price.

Does He know what He's doing? Absolutely. He knows the path to death's door because He voluntarily walked through it and was in complete control of the moment it came for Him (John 10:18, Luke 23:46). He knows precisely how to separate our spirit from our body, slip us out of earth's body bag, and sail us past the Southern Cross and Crown Nebula into the harbor of heaven. He is our Great and Faithful Guide and we have His Word He will get us there (John 14:1-4).

Is He trustworthy? He willingly gave Himself as the Great and Perfect Sacrifice for our sin so it would no longer be an obstacle to our relationship with Him (Mark 10:45, Ephesians 2:1-7). If He was willing to suffer the torture of man's hatred and the Father's rejection to achieve that, need we even ask if He can be trusted to ferry us to heaven and invest us with a new body which reflects the glory of His own? Which is harder? Which requires more pain and suffering? If He's willing to do the harder thing, how much more the joyful task of liberating us from our "earthly tent" so what is mortal and infirmed is swallowed up by immortality and life (1 Corinthians 15:42-50, 2 Corinthians 5:1-5)?

Is the cost He charges fair?

Is it fair?

No.

It is not fair.

It's *free.*

What we've covered before bears repeating: Jesus Christ's entire mission on earth was to let us know our sin renders us paralyzed to do anything which warrants God's acceptance based on our virtue, dedication, commitment, or self-assessed sincerity.

His love for us drove Him to do everything required to redeem us. He *wanted* to offer the perfect sacrifice to erase our sin. He *wanted* to conquer sin and death through resurrection. He *wants to* share the benefits of that victory with us. No other human being has ever done that. None ever will. He has no hidden agenda or malicious intent to manipulate us so we feel unworthy of what He did. His sole purpose was to show us how much we're worth to Him. The Holy Spirit inspired the apostle Peter to put it this way:

> For you know it was not with perishable things such as
> silver or gold that you were redeemed from the empty
> way of life handed down to you from your forefathers,
> but with the precious blood of Christ, a lamb with-
> out blemish or defect.

1 PETER 1:18-19, NIV

We were given the *imago dei* ("image of God") at conception and Jesus Christ means to perfect it—completely and eternally. When we placed our faith in Him, He made a willful, rock-solid, never-changing commitment to view us as if our sin never existed—including its effect on our bodies. He's been preparing us for the Grand Unveiling ever since (Romans 3:21-26, 4:22-25, 5:9, 8:1, 1 Corinthians 1:30, 15:42-43, 2 Corinthians 5:21, Philippians 3:20-21, Titus 3:5-7).

To put it another way, our present weaknesses are a reminder of sin, yes, but more importantly, *they're a reminder of the sin He's preparing us to leave behind.* Days littered with aches and pains, fear, apprehension, and vulnerability need only remind us there is *none of that* where we're going. We can live in the promise our "one day" has always been greater than our present day. Until then, He's at our side, using the prep work for our departure as a way to show others what "[His] power perfected in weakness" looks like (2 Corinthians 12:9-10). Which means He's calling us to stand resolute and confident *our final days, no matter how bedridden they seem, are unique days* because they put some remarkable truths on display as He readies us for the journey home.

"Such as?" we may ask. Good question. Let's start with an icon in the middle of New York Harbor...

Chapter 11

WE'RE GETTING READY

Part Two

I sat on the front row, waiting for the impossible. I'd seen a television version of what was about to unfold a few years before but everyone knows TV specializes in next level smoke-and-mirror deception. Use multiple cameras, just the right lighting, and a computer with all the processing speed you could ever want—and you can make a Longhorn look like he's blowing "Taps."

This was different. This was live—as in on the church platform thirty feet away, from which I'd shared hundreds of messages as pastor. That dude up there, one of the world's great illusionists, the one who advised his friend and fellow world-renowned illusionist on the television version of what we were about to see, was going to make a ten-foot replica of the Statue of Liberty disappear before hundreds.

Curious to watch the set up, I arrived an hour or so before showtime. The crew was busy putting a crate here and a prop there but it seemed pretty routine. Granted, there were a few moments when the church staff and volunteers were asked to leave the auditorium—but when we returned, everything looked the same. The show was tremendous and as it moved to the finale, excitement grew. Finally, there she was: Lady Liberty herself. Front and center, tablet and torch in hand, looking resplendent.

After a bit of theatrics to build tension, the stage crew pulled what looked like a circular shower curtain up and over her head. Three or four seconds later, they dropped it like an ant-infested pair of hiking shorts ... and Lady Liberty was gone. And friends, I do mean *completely gone.* As in, *disappeared without a trace.*

Please understand. The church stage was a fully carpeted wood-framed structure three feet above a solid cement floor. There was no trap door. The carpeted choir loft was built into the stage, guarded on both sides and at the back by a forty foot wall, with one 4' x 7' door on either side and no baptistry. Aside from those doors, the only other way to exit the stage was down three steps at the front to the main floor. All of which meant Lady Liberty had *nowhere* to go. But Lady Liberty had gone bye-bye.

Like the rest of the crowd, I was stunned. I thought for sure my seat to the left of center stage would allow me to see how they did it. Not a chance. I was equally dumbfounded when, after about twenty seconds of dazed, childlike awe, the shower curtain was lifted and dropped just as quickly—and there stood Lady Liberty again.

That was some illusion.

Jesus Christ once asked His beloved friend Martha, "I am the resurrection and the life; he who believes in Me will live even if he dies; and everyone who lives and believes in Me will never die. Do you believe this?" (John 11:25-26).

Note the way He put it. First, we will live even if we die, insinuating we die first, then live again. He could have stopped right there. "Right, Lord. Death and taxes. Got it. It's all around us. We live, we die; that's life."

Yet the next phrase seems a startling contradiction to what He'd just said. He told Martha the person who believes in Him will *never* die. "Wait a minute, Lord. Which is it? Do we die or don't we? You just said we die then we live. Now you're saying we don't die. How can we die, not die, and live all at the same time? That's just not possible..."

Unless...

Death isn't what it seems. It may look like the end. It may appear real to those standing next to our bedside, coffin, urn—or church platform. But with Jesus Christ, looks can be deceiving. In fact, looks *are* deceiving. A believer's dead body is a mirage, one the enemy wants to slather with his specialized brand of deceit, persuading us to check faith at the door and believe what we see is what we've got. It's done. It's over. There is no more.

Yet Jesus' words assure us nothing could be further from the truth. Death is life's greatest illusion; so much so it can be spoken of as if doesn't exist. Just as a shadow is the absence of light and the presence of nothing, aging and death are specters of falsehood masquerading as the truth. We don't stop being who we are. We don't become nothing. We go from weakness to perfection as seamlessly as Lady Liberty stood before us once again.

That's because He already sees what we will be, remember? His view of the future is the same as His view of the present and the past. One view from the Eternal One in which there is no break, interruption, discontinuity, disruption, or misstep. What we were will instantaneously meld into what we've always been in His eyes. All the lessons He's taught us and experiences He's taken us through, all the molding and chiseling He's done to give us wisdom and insight, will be instantly energized into singular, timeless perfection.

As noted in chapter two, it's why David king of Israel could say, "Even though I walk through the valley of the *shadow* of death, I fear no evil, for You are with me; Your rod and Your staff, they comfort me" (Psalm 23:4, emphasis mine). He called it a shadow for a reason. He understood death isn't the moment infirmities win the day and sin separates us from Him—it's the moment all that is vaporized and we join Him forever.

Is our faith weak if we fear what may kill us? Of course not. ALS makes for a difficult end to life here. So does Parkinson's, multiple sclerosis, pancreatic cancer, and stroke. Even David had moments when the fear of "death" got the best of him:

> My heart is in anguish within me and the terrors of death have fallen upon me. Fear and trembling come upon me and horror has overwhelmed me. I said, "Oh, that I had wings like a dove! I would fly away and be at rest ..."
>
> PSALM 55:4-6

Yet somewhere along the way, David learned the anguished terror of "death" *must* bow the knee to "Surely goodness and lovingkindness will follow me all the days of my life, and I will dwell in the house of the Lord forever" (Psalm 23:6). He learned every troubling, fearful, anxiety-ridden experience ultimately ends in God's goodness and love winning the day. The end of life here is no different. The Deep Six (compassion, grace, patience, loyal love, truth, and justice) win again.[9]

---

9. Read Psalm 56:2-4 for extra encouragement.

Through Jesus Christ's Love and Power—and through His willingness to taste death for everyone (meaning bodily agony and separation from God as punishment for sin, see Hebrews 2:9)—we really do cheat the hangman. We lose nothing and gain everything, just as He did when He left earth and regained the glory He had with God the Father before the world existed (John 17:5, Acts 1:9-11). I'm even convinced I'll get my hair back.

Jesus Christ readying us for departure means comfort in knowing death isn't death. It also platforms another remarkable truth.

HE WILL REMEMBER US EVEN IF WE DON'T

The path we must walk to physical perfection may not be welcome news but it's bearable—if our minds stay put. After all, we can converse from a walker or pray from a wheelchair; and a well-timed word of encouragement can embrace a hurting heart even if our arms can't. But what if God's plan involves some form of dementia which robs us of rational thought and strips away memories, leaving us less than we've ever been?

That's why we talked about who's in charge of our self-image in chapter four. A faltering mind is the ultimate test of whether we believe our image rests with Him or ourselves and others. If it's the latter, we have little more to look forward to than shards of despair tearing through us as our personality and memories splinter. If it's the former, we can rest assured a wandering mind does not map our course to eternity. His mind—depthless, eternal, and perfect–does.

That doesn't mean He'll miraculously reverse dementia's effect so we can read a clockface, tell the doctor who is President, know our loved ones, or distinguish a penny from a dime. It does mean

He will not forget who we are—even when we do. Like everything else in the Christian life, *our future perfection does not depend on us—or what's left of us.* He *will* deliver what He's promised, that is, all of who we are to heaven to be with Him forever. Dementia will die. We will not.

Romans 2:15-16 provides an important glimpse. Referring to those who have not heard the gospel, the Spirit, through Paul, says at Judgment Day they will...

> ...show the work of the Law written in their hearts, their *conscience* bearing witness and their *thoughts* alternately accusing or else defending them on the day when, according to my gospel, God will judge the secrets of men through Christ Jesus (emphasis mine).

If dementia permanently robs unbelievers of memories, thought, language, attention, and consciousness before they die, how can God use what no longer exists to judge them? Simply put, He won't. The Spirit is clear what they may have forgotten—or what dementia may have temporarily taken away—will be reinstalled into their consciousness. Who they fully were will be who they are again. Then God will judge their secrets—including every careless word they ever uttered—resulting in a tragic outcome (Matthew 10:28, 12:36-37, Romans 2:12-16, Revelation 20:11-15).

Believers in Jesus Christ need never fear that judgment. We are His, the penalty for our sin has been taken care of, He has promised us heaven, and no power in heaven or hell can snatch us from His hand (John 3:16, 5:24, 10:28-29, Romans 3:21-26, 4:16-25, Hebrews 10:12-14, 1 Peter 3:18).

But like unbelievers, what dementia may have robbed He will restore. We will be fully us again—bodies, minds, hearts, souls, and personalities in full, redemptive regalia—not to be condemned but to joyfully enter His kingdom and receive His abundantly gracious reward for faithful service (Matthew 25:14-30, 34, Luke 12:32, 19:12-27, 1 Corinthians 3:10-15, 2 Corinthians 5:10).

If dementia or some other debilitating disease is gaining ground in your life, those around you need to know that though your mind and body are fading, your love for Him and them is not. They also need to know despite what's happening to you, His love for you and them is more constant than the consecutive lifetime of a billion suns.

Encourage them to remember the temporal cannot rob the eternal, He conquered death and so will you, the road there may seem long and tortuous but is, in fact, just a moment; you are confident He will skillfully shepherd you home (Ps. 116:15, Isaiah 46:3-4), when you step through death into eternal life, you won't care about how you got there and neither should they, and assure them you will be with Him, He will be with them, and one day, you will all be together again.

Here's another unique truth the end of days brings...

DEATH IS THE FINAL
WAY WE GLORIFY GOD

As mentioned before, this may seem incompatible with His claim to be the God of the living (Matthew 22:32). How can a God who claims to be the source of life be glorified by its opposite? More specifically, how is He glorified by allowing *His people* to endure the dying process?

This is a good place to correct any misunderstandings about what it means for God to seek His own glory. He's not an egomaniac on a quest to do what's best for Him with no regard for us. If that were the case, the waves of Noah's flood would still be slapping high-fives over Mount Everest and His One eternal thought about us would be "good-bye and good riddance."

His glory isn't about a private motorcade speeding Him to the arena, standing on stage in the spotlight while people scream His name, then being whisked away to the after-party while the *hoi polloi* fight crowds and traffic to get home. Nor is it about how many followers He has, how many trophies clutter His shelves, or how much face-time He's getting in front of the camera. That's the world's measure of fame; and we're so bombarded with it we think that's what He's like, too.

On the contrary, history is embossed with an altogether different mark of His glory: the overwhelming Selflessness of the Cross. In other words, His glory is about a relentless drive to engineer our lives so we and the people around us are the eternal beneficiaries of His compassion, grace, patience, loyal love, truth, and justice (the Deep Six). Glorifying Him in death is our last—and many times, most powerful—opportunity to partner with Him in putting the Deep Six on display.

That's not a bad gig if our final days mean being at home in minimal pain surrounded by friends and loved ones. Or even better, if we conclude a bible study at 9 p.m. by talking about how good He is, then slip away to heaven at 2:00 a.m. while dead asleep. But what happens if the hall monitors to heaven are cancer, heart disease, TIA's, or a hundred other illnesses that make death seem worse than landing on an aircraft carrier in thirty-foot seas? How in the world does a death like *that* put the Deep Six on display?

I'm sure the apostle Peter wondered the same thing. None of us would relish hearing one of the last things Jesus said to him. Following Peter's betrayal, the Lord reinstated him to ministry by commanding him three times to love His people. Then He said:

> Truly, truly, I say to you, when you were younger, you used to gird yourself and walk wherever you wished; but when you grow old, you will stretch out your hands and someone else will lead you where you do not wish to go. Now this He said, signifying by what kind of death he would glorify God. And when He had spoken this, He said to him, "Follow Me."
>
> JOHN 21:18-19

The Lord didn't provide details. He didn't give Peter a procedures manual for what to do or say when this or that happened. He gave him a prediction and a command. It was up to Peter, with His Master at his side, to live under the strain of *the now and the not yet*, trusting the Deep Six would best be displayed by something other than blissfully drifting into heaven while counting sheep. Church tradition says he was crucified, some say upside down. We can't know for sure. Regardless, it was his final turn at "letting the Lord have his tension . . . please."

Death is our final turn, too, trusting no matter what the circumstances, the Deep Six will show up in at least three ways. One, they will be there when family and friends count it a privilege to comfort us in affliction, weep with us, and assist in bearing our burden, fulfilling the law of Christ (Romans 12:15, 2 Corinthians 1:3-7, Galatians 6:2).

During my years as a pastor, a church leader told me of a family who gathered with their husband and father, hospitalized in his last hours. It was hard for everyone; for him as he fought to hang on and for them as they watched him struggle.

During their vigil, someone placed a chair next to his bed. At one point, one of his children leaned over to him and said, "You know Dad, it's OK to go home. Jesus is here. He's sitting right next to you in this chair." A few minutes later the family stepped out of the room for a break. When they returned, they discovered their husband and dad had leaned over, put his head on the arm of that chair, and gone home.

Selfless words of comfort, assurance, and love, spoken with his best interest at heart, assured him there was no need to struggle any longer. His family gave him permission not to worry about them, to be at peace, and to finally go home with The One Who'd been sitting in the chair next to him his whole life.

Two, the Deep Six show up by demonstrating when bodies fail, Jesus does not. He knows what it's like to feel life ebbing from this edifice of flesh and bone. It's why Psalm 116:15 is such a magnificent verse: "Precious in the sight of the Lord is the death of His godly ones." The Old Testament Hebrew word for "precious" often described jewels used to build the Temple or found in a king's crown (2 Samuel 12:30, 1 Kings 7:9-11). It's also used in Isaiah's prophecy of the Messiah, describing Him as a "costly cornerstone" (Isaiah 28:16).

It's meaning here tells us in our waning moments, He sits in the chair doting over us, taking great pains as one would care for a jewel of great value, ready to separate the mortal from the immortal and clothe us with the eternal when we finally rest in Him. As we've seen, He dismantled one precious Temple, raised one even more precious (His body, John 2:19-21), and in His *tour de force,* will do the same for everyone who believes in Him.

Remember also those watching are more than the eye can see.

The Holy Spirit reminds us angels are commissioned by God to serve Christians (Psalm 104:4, Hebrews 1:14). They routinely observe us and are involved in our care—and long to watch His gracious plan for us unfold (1 Peter 1:12). Also, Christ's public display and disarmament of the rulers and authorities at His crucifixion likely refers to human and demonic czars who watched helplessly as He eviscerated their eternal power (Colossians 2:15). What better way to rub salt in the wound than command they observe the Deep Six triumph in each of us on the journey home?

Three, God's glory is seen when dying faith is expressed and shared with others. Do not forget when death comes knocking, the gospel knocks with it. Our final days may be the greatest opportunity we have to share the words of Life with others. Never underestimate how hard it is for a friend, nurse, doctor, lab technician, or family member to discount or ignore dying faith.

The world has no clue where that kind of hope comes from— yet they want it, desperately. Don't discount that trust and peace in eyes flickering to sleep here and flaming to life there are powerful beacons of the gospel. He can easily look through them into someone's soul and bring them to faith. Think of how remarkable it will be to see believers in heaven who were unbelievers with whom we shared the gospel during our final days.

There is at least one more way His getting us ready for Life can make our final days, unique days. It's centers on remembering…

AFTER WE'RE ALL SAID AND DONE … HE'S NOT ALL SAID AND DONE

We've mentioned David, king of Israel. Review his life and one easily discovers he displayed moments of great nobility and godliness. He killed Goliath to defend God's honor, graciously spared

Saul's life despite his repeated attempts to kill David, assembled everything necessary to build the Temple, and wrote "A perverse heart shall depart from me; I will know no evil" (1 Samuel 17, 24, 26, 1 Chronicles 22-29, Psalm 101:4).

But one just as easily discovers he had a dark side that almost defies description. When his trust in God's protection from Saul faltered, he formed an alliance with Israel's enemies—even raiding his own countrymen to win their favor. He committed adultery and murdered the husband of his paramour. He brought about the genocide of 70,000 men in Israel by taking a census of his army against God's wishes (1 Samuel 27, 2 Samuel 11, 12, 24, 1 Chronicles 21). Yeah boy, that David, he was some kinda…

… man after God's own heart.

Those are God's gracious words, not mine. You can read them for yourself in 1 Samuel 13:14. Never mind they were spoken before any of the sins mentioned above happened. God knew what he'd do and said it anyway because He'd snapped a chalk line of grace across David's eternity. No power in heaven or hell (or failure on David's part) could smear it, smudge it, or wipe it away.

David knew that—and God knew he knew it—and that's why He called him a man after His own heart. Clearly, David wasn't more obedient than anyone else. He just knew every time he sinned and repented, God's grace would be as limitless as He is—a promise that's true for all whose faith rests in Him (Psalm 32:1-7, 103:3, 10-14, 130:3-4, Isaiah 1:18, Micah 7:18-20, Matthew 18:21-22, 1 Timothy 1:15-17, Hebrews 10:12-18, 1 John 1:9).

That said, I doubt even David understood how far the Lord is willing to take it. Yet the Old Testament is clear: His grace is so limitless that even after David "died," God blessed future generations of Israelites for his sake (1 Kings 11:13, 32, 34, 15:1-5, Psalm 89:20-37, 132:10-12, Isaiah 37:33-35, Jeremiah 33:19-22). He's done the same for the Jewish patriarchs Abraham, Isaac, and Jacob. Along with David, they arrived in heaven and discovered God's grace to them would unfold in the lives of those they left behind (compare Deuteronomy 29:13-15 and 30:20 with Romans 11:25-29; and see Matthew 22:31-32, Mark 12:26-37, Luke 20:37-38, and John 8:56-58).[10]

Believers in this age should look forward to that promise, too. If you have any doubts about that, remember we've experienced greater levels of grace *right now* than Old Testament believers did while on earth. We know the mystery of the gospel's full truth and power, "Christ in us, the hope of glory" (Colossians 1:26-27; see also Romans 16:25-26, 1 Corinthians 2:7, Ephesians 1:3, 3:8-10, Colossians 3:3-4, Hebrews 12:18-24). We believe in One we've never seen—and Jesus says we are blessed because we do (John 20:29).

Each of us is permanently indwelled and sealed with the Holy Spirit, Who has given us at least one supernatural gift to glorify God and serve others (Luke 11:13, 1 Corinthians 12, 2 Corinthians 1:21-22, Ephesians 1:13-14, 1 Peter 4:10-11). Unlike the Old Testament priesthood (which was reserved for Aaron's descendants), *every* Christian is a member of God's royal priesthood (Exodus 28:40-41, 1 Peter 2:9-10). Further, the lessons learned about His character by people in the Old Testament were for our benefit, "upon whom the ends of the ages have come" (1 Corinthians 10:11).

Old Testament believers couldn't claim any of those privileges—at least not permanently. (The Holy Spirit's work in David is an exception, see 1 Samuel 16:13). In fact, Jesus told his disciples

---

10. I don't mean to imply people in heaven are able to look in on people they've known here. The Bible doesn't teach that. I simply mean that, just as martyred believers in heaven are generally aware God has not yet exercised His full wrath against humanity's sin (Revelation 6:9-11), it seems reasonable we will have a greater general understanding of how God's faithfulness to us is being expressed on earth.

many prophets and kings wished to experience what we do, yet never did (Luke 10:23-24). Even now, they await the New Heavens and New Earth because it cannot come to pass until we're ready to inherit it with them (Isaiah 66:22-23, Hebrews 11:39-40, Revelation 21:1-2). In other words, if God's blessings to those left behind was true of the grace Old Testament believers received, how much more is it true of the Greater Grace we have in Christ?

All of that to say His faithfulness to others for our sake doesn't die when our heart stops beating. True, generations here must remain faithful to enjoy His blessings (Deuteronomy 7:9, 12, 28:1-14, Ezekiel 18:20). What a man or woman sows, he or she reaps (Proverbs 11:18, 22:8, Galatians 6:7-8). At the same time, this principle is in play. How He balances the two is one of the great mysteries of His Grace.

The takeaway is when we're all said and done, *He's* not all said and done. He's limitless so He can't be. If waning bodies and receding minds make it seem otherwise, we should chalk that up to another of the enemy's lies. The truth is, we're rapidly shedding the weight of imperfection so we can sprint faster to the day we're ageless and perfect—and Jesus Christ can ratchet His grace up another notch by displaying it in others' lives for our sake. If there are more meaningful days than that, *please.* Tell me what they are.

Still, The Wall we've mentioned looms—and everyone must climb it. Every. One. No exceptions, no passes for good behavior, no promises 180 pounds of chiseled, twenty-something masculinity or 125 pounds of homecoming queen won't end up as 95 pounds of bed-ridden memories.

If you're like me, the first thing that comes to mind—especially when you remember people you've known and loved who have gone through all that—is death stinks.

Chapter 12

DEATH STINKS

L iterally.

Martha of Bethany knew that. We don't know *how* but apparently somewhere in her earthly sojourn she encountered dead bodies. She learned once life leaves a corpse, biomechanical mechanisms responsible for sustenance and renewal seize up in contaminated quagmires of decay. Left unattended, the result can make a stock yard smell like a rose garden.

That's why some cultures bury within twenty-four hours, others wrap bodies in spice and perfume, and others embalm and adorn with makeup. It's our last chance for a bit of image management, doing what we have always done, seeking to convince others we are not what everyone knows we are. After those trained to handle such matters have done so, there's nothing left to do but bury it, walk away, and leave dead enough alone.

It's also why we can sympathize with Martha's objection to Jesus Christ's troubling proposal to open the tomb where her dead brother, Lazarus—the friend Jesus loved—had been for four days (John 11:35-36, 39).

Though the text doesn't tell us, Martha and her sister, Mary, may have helped with burial preparations. It's what good sisters would have done. But it would have been difficult. Tears likely fell as they touched skin, once warm and supple, and realized death really is cold as hell. Eyes which once looked at them with laughter and life were now closed, a mouth which once creased Lazarus' face with smiles and crow's feet now flatlined across a lifeless countenance. As preparations came to a close, what was left of their brother was wrapped up and sealed off. Head to toe, the burial cloth did away with anything which would have reminded anyone of Lazarus of Bethany.

He's dead.

And it stinks.

Would any of us want to see—and smell—a loved one in that condition? Would any of us want *that* memory to be our last? "For God's sake, Jesus, please. Please don't. Just leave him alone."

Just leave him alone? For God's sake? Is that what Jesus Christ does? He just leaves people He loves alone when they die—for God's sake?

> Jesus said to her, "Did I not say to you if you believe, you will see the glory of God?" So they removed the stone. Then Jesus raised His eyes, and said, "Father, I thank You that You have heard Me. I know You always hear Me; but because of the people standing around I said it, so they may believe You sent Me."
>
> JOHN 11:40-42

Note those with Martha and Mary complied with His request to remove the stone covering his tomb (v. 39)—an act of faith any pastor worth his salt could shape into a fine sermon. For time's sake, I'll let your inner preacher handle that.

More to the point, note He *was* acting for God's sake. He and His heavenly Father had talked about this. The Son, whose will is always in line with the Father's (Luke 22:42, John 4:34, 5:30, 6:38) made a request He knew the Father would grant because what better way to display His compassion, grace, patience, loyal-love, truth, and justice (the Deep Six) than at a tomb? Lazarus' body had been buried. God's Power, Character, and Love had not.

> When He had said these things, He cried out with a loud voice, "Lazarus, come forth." The man who had died came forth, bound hand and foot with wrappings, and his face was wrapped around with a cloth. Jesus said to them, "Unbind him, and let him go."
>
> JOHN 11:43-44

Hammer, anvil, and stirrup beat their rhythms again. Sound waves rippled inside the cochlea. Electric impulses darted along auditory nerves to 100 billion brain cells spontaneously jump-started and sustained by six billion volts.[11] Lungs drew air like jet engines. The heart squeezed blood, moments before congealed in infested, stagnant pools along 60,000 miles of rotting causeway, to every cell, toxin free.[12] Muscle memory remembered. Atrophy flexed. Lazarus, dressed in life again, heard his Friend's voice, sat up, and walked out of his tomb.

There was no stench. Tears of joy fell on skin, warm and supple once more. Eyes danced with laughter and life; smiles and crow's feet put their arms around each other. Everything wrapped up and sealed off was unwrapped and unveiled. Head to toe, the burial cloth revealed everything. Lazarus of Bethany was alive.

---

11. *Popular Science*, Spring, 2018, p. 6.
12. https://my.clevelandclinic.org/health/articles/17059-how-does-blood-flow-through-your-body

What had been, then wasn't, was once again. Jesus Christ had done the impossible. Just as He did at creation, He raced into chaos and death and infused the dust of a human body with so much life there was no sign it had ever died. He proved, as He had with the centurion's slave and Jairus' daughter, Lazarus' death was no match for Him (Luke 7:1-10, Mark 5:21-43). Ours won't be either.

The crowd's reaction is understandable. They saw and believed (John 11:45). Whether they realized it or not, at that moment they stepped out of their graves and took their place next to Lazarus. His experience became their promise. Whatever happened between then and their death had no bearing on their eternal destiny. Yes, age would come, their bodies would falter, and one day they'd be wrapped in swaddling cloths and laid in a tomb. But the Baby from the manger, The One Who knew the path from birth through death to new life, would be there to shepherd them home.

One day, when you and I enter His kingdom, what we looked and felt like the moment we died will be so radically altered we'll remember nothing of oxygen tanks, rheumatoid arthritis, and arteriosclerosis. We will remember only we *were* old. The details will be irrelevant. We'll hear His voice, loud and strong, telling death to let go. Death will listen. By His command, our soul will be clothed with bones, sinews, and skin once again—made just for us, made just like us (Job 19:25-27, Isaiah 26:19, 1 Corinthians 15:35-57, 1 John 3:2).

We will see each other as we were always intended, with the smears of sin and imperfection wiped from the canvas. Each of us unique. Each of us special. Each of us an eternal original, bearing no mark of age or imperfection, showing what we'd always hoped we could be—in mind, body, soul, and spirit—but could never become while here. Never mind it took a lifetime to get there. He'll remedy that in an instant. It will be the great moment of the great promise: Death swallowed up in victory (1 Corinthians 15:54-57). When the moment comes, He may well explain why our form of aging and death was entrusted to us. Why did He assign Alzheimer's to my dad and cancer to my fifteen-year-old niece? Why did your ninety-year-old father come in from a morning's yard work, sit down with a glass of iced tea, and die peacefully—and your best friend struggle for a decade with type-1 diabetes? Not that loved ones in heaven sit around wondering about it. It's either been explained to them and they get it or they're so swept up in an ageless heaven they don't care.

Of this I am sure: we'll realize it was worth the wait. Like children tortured Christmas morning "will never get here," the joy of its arrival will obliterate the pain and drudgery of its delay. Sleeplessness at 2 a.m. will give way to senses filled with the sights and sounds of the eternal moment. We'll see what's been planned for us all along and be utterly amazed at how comprehensive, consuming, immaculate, and flawless it is. The imperfections of this *age* will have served their role to make the moment all the sweeter. Having done so, they'll be tossed aside like bows and wrapping paper—because that's all they ever were. The shroud is discarded, the gift remains.

Forever.

Chapter 13

THE FUTURE AWAITS

I hate that I can't read a menu anymore and when my order arrives, the food is blurry. Ditto for needing reading glasses to undo a twist tie. Then there's forgetting what I needed upstairs by the time I reach downstairs to look for it. It's harder to find just the right word when conversing. I don't remember things as easily. The fast twitch muscles which once powered me to the title of the fastest kid in my elementary school hitch as much as they twitch these days.

I don't sleep as well as I used to and I run out of gas every day around dinner. My hearing is still acute and I'm thankful—but I'm well aware the day may come when music or a bird's sonnet won't seem as sweet. Likewise for the savory goodness of teriyaki salmon, a fine cup of coffee, fresh fruit, sushi, virtually anything chocolate, and the-out-of-this-world goodness of a honey-baked ham or pulled-pork barbecue.

The day may also come when my mind throws a penalty flag on the play on words which still come naturally—or on thoughts flowing from the Spirit to my fingertips in streams of articulation which make me realize *there's no way I came up with that.* Rather than the grand, sweeping "S" I make to start my signature, an 'X' may one day be a touchdown of penmanship.

But it is not lost on me—and should not be on you—that with Jesus Christ imaging life's MRI, things which abate here are simply promissory notes on our future. Our eyesight dims because we no longer need to see this world as clearly. We're being prepared to see something greater, a world which luminesces with a clarity and beauty like nothing we can imagine. Our hearing abates because it's being reconfigured to access frequencies carrying the voice of God and the praise of angels. Our lack of appetite means we're losing our taste for anything other than the magnificent feasts of heaven. Touch and smell aren't as acute because they are about to be replaced with sensory capacity that would blow every earth-bound, neurological circuit we have.

Muscles, bones, tendons, ligaments, and reflexes are being benched because a new you is being woven together, one who will do things in heaven—and on the earth when you return with Jesus Christ to establish His kingdom—you can only dream about. In other words, your energy and abilities here are being emptied so they can be replaced in the future with Spirit-driven enablement which knows no end.

Biblical glimpses are not hard to find. Samson killed one thousand men with a donkey's jawbone and carried Gaza's city gate (its doors, two posts, and bars) on his shoulders 38 miles to the top of a mountain opposite Hebron (Judges 15:15-16, 16:3). Daniel and his three friends stood with the Lord in a furnace so hot it killed those who threw them in. When they stepped out, they didn't even smell like smoke (Daniel 3:13-27, Isaiah 43:1-2).

David killed Goliath (who was over nine feet tall and carried a spear weighing around thirty two pounds) with a slingshot and one swipe of his sword. When he fled for his life from king Saul, he described his God-empowered abilities as overtaking an army and leaping over a wall—a metaphorical picture, I believe, of the abilities we will have in the future. Ditto for Isaiah's description of the strength gained by those who wait for the Lord. Elijah was empowered to outrun Ahab's chariot seventeen miles to Jezreel. Our Lord walked on water, enabled Peter to do the same, and transgressed walls and closed doors in His resurrection body (1 Samuel 17:1-51, 1 Kings 18:46, Psalm 18:29, Isaiah 40:29-31, Matthew 14:22-33, John 20:19).

Given the evidence, it is not hard to imagine our service to Him when we return here—and in eternity beyond—will be an explosive expansion of human potential which rivals the creation of the universe. Imagine, if you can, the cosmic inflation of human ingenuity, creative genius, and physical prowess—integrated with quantum levels of integrity and moral purity—which will be unleashed when we get to finally do what we were made to do. Saturn will call out to Alpha Centauri to hang on to something "because this is going to be epic" (Romans 8:20-23).

"Hi, I need a space ship to tour the galaxy. Can't wait to get out there and marvel at what He's made. Would love it with a clear bubble top like one of those George Jetson cars and fins like a '59 Cadillac Eldorado."

"What color?"

"Was thinking of a two-toner. Maybe something in starlight blue with ruby red accents."

"Nice. Two seater?"

"Uh, four … if it's not too much trouble."

"Yeah, we can do that for ya. Pickup this Friday work for you?"

"The two of you want me to do *what?*"

"You heard me. He thinks it's a great idea."

"You want me to recompose Mozart's piano concerto in B flat major?"

"Yes. We thought a new twist on an ol' standard might be nice. And yes, we're well aware you've only been playing a month. But He's given you quite a gift so you oughta be playin' 'Chopsticks' in two octaves with one hand tied behind your back by now."

"Funny you should mention that. Why just last week I …"

"Well, there you go! Time to start tickling those ivories for Him. He looks forward to hearing you play; everyone's invited. He says you'll knock the Steinway out of the park and uh, you've probably noticed, He is *never* wrong. So time to score one for the Savior. Get it? *Score one?* As in write a musical score? Ha!"

"Oh, and one more thing … David wants to sit in on harp so see what you can do to work him in for a few bars."

In such a world, it is not too far a stretch to imagine we will swim with dolphins in the Mediterranean or climb Mt. Everest in an afternoon. How about a picnic lunch in the Rockies followed by an early dinner in Key West—with no need for jets or bullet trains to make the trip? Or a fellowship breakfast with the Lord on Mt. Sinai followed by a Q&A with Moses? Then it's off to Norway to watch the Aurora Borealis set to music as angels sing of His glory. As we saw in chapter nine, eternal life with Him will be the perfect balance between service, praise, and recreation, all of it an act of worship, as human existence was always intended (Psalm 79:13, 115:17-18, 145:21, Romans 12:1-2).

As for the stopper being pulled on our minds and memories, take heart what's being drained away now is about to be filled with new words and memories so grand and electrifying there's no room for recollections of things here (Isaiah 65:17).

After all, as much as we wish it were different, every memory, impression, intuition, or bit of knowledge in this world is tainted with some degree of sin and imperfection. The concert was great—but not perfect. The dissertation was adequate but not outstanding. The trip to Hawaii was wonderful—but there were hassles with the luggage and that argument over the shopping spree dulled some of its luster—as did the three years it took to pay off the credit cards. The kids… well, let's just say videos of adorable three-year-olds tend to turn into teenage horror films. Then there are taxes, politics, car repairs, leaking roofs, and a thousand other imperfections which remind us the world we dreamed of in our youth never existed. That's why we're being re-calibrated for another.

As Daniel approached the end of his life, God sent him an angelic messenger to unfold a great panorama of human history (Daniel 10-12). At the end of that revelation, the angel told him of a resurrection to eternal life in which people "will shine brightly like the brightness of the expanse of heaven, and those who lead the many to righteousness like the stars forever and ever" (12:2-3). Does that sound like an existence where any part of our mind, spirit, or body will show *any* sign of imperfection?

It reminds us that from before the beginning, God has intended to rip the coffin lid off the sin we've encased ourselves in. It started when He shed the blood of an animal to cover Adam and Eve's sin (see chapter four). It continued when He enabled them (and us) to create and perpetuate imperfect life (Genesis 3:15, 20-21, and 4:1)—which He would not have done if He didn't intend to ultimately dress us in Christ's perfection.

When Moses died on Mount Nebo, Satan and Michael the Archangel had an argument over who should get the body because Satan knew resurrection was in the wings (Deuteronomy 34:1-6, Jude 9). What better way to spoil the party than for the body of the Lawgiver to be AWOL when God sounded the call for "dead" believers to rise from their graves (1 Corinthians 15:51-57, 1 Thessalonians 4:13-18)? It would have been the ultimate irony: Sin, revealed by the Law through the Lawgiver, would have claimed an important victim and pinned Grace and Truth to the mat. So he stood there, with a sick smirk on his face I'm sure, demanding Moses' body with the same vehemence as the permission he sought to sift Jesus' disciples like wheat (Luke 22:31).

He lost the argument. God took care of Moses' body and fifteen hundred years later, placed him on the Mount of Transfiguration with no ill effects of his death or disobedience (Matthew 17:1-8, Mark 9:2-8, Luke 9:28-36). All of it had been redeemed—a reminder God has no intention of letting past sins mar, disfigure, or diminish our future. The prophet Elijah, who did not die but was taken to heaven in a whirlwind, was there, too (2 Kings 2:11). So was The One Who called Himself "the Resurrection and the Life," proving He delivers on the promise whoever believes in Him will never die (John 11:25-26, 2 Peter 1:17-18).

≈≈≈

If you take a moment to review the passage in Luke 9:28-36, note Moses and Elijah weren't seated silently at Jesus' feet, feverishly scribbling notes on metaphysiology, dimensional modalities, or the physics of prophecy. They were *talking with* Him; that is, enjoying a free exchange of thoughts and ideas about what He would accomplish in Jerusalem. That's what human perfection and divine engagement looks like. Prayer is practice for it; resurrection will be the perfect embodiment of it.

Also notice there is no mention of how *old* Moses and Elijah looked. It was—and is—irrelevant. Along the same lines, consider this: Jesus Christ, in His humanity, is over 2,000 years old. Do any of us think He looks it? Sin cannot touch Him where He is, which means age and infirmity cannot touch Him. In His present state, He is the supreme physical expression of the Lamb "unblemished and spotless," forever displaying the perfection which qualified Him to be the substitute for our sin (1 Peter 1:18-19).

He has no wrinkles or age spots, no midriff bulge, and no need for bifocals. "Diabetes" "dementia," "cancer," and "coronary artery disease" aren't even words in heaven, much less expressions of His physical condition. He has not "lost a step" nor does His memory lapse in any way, shape, or form.[13] He is, in every sense of the phrase, a perfect Human Being.

---

13. That, by the way, is why we can trust Him to help when tough times parade through our lives or temptation pounds on the door. He remembers perfectly what it's like to face them and knows exactly how to help us (see Hebrews 2:16-18 and 4:14-16).

Consider also Mary's encounter with Him outside the tomb on Resurrection Day. She thought He was the gardener (John 20:14-15). That's only reasonable if He showed no effects of the brutal abuse He suffered two days before (Isaiah 52:14, 53:5, Matthew 27:26-27:50, Mark 14:65-15:37, Luke 22:63-23:46, John 19). Ditto for His encounter with two disciples on the road to Emmaus (Luke 24:13-35). It's clear from both appearances He was in His resurrection body. It had been redeemed, restored, and re-created. The devils' henchmen had been dismissed, the effects of sin were gone, and every bit of His humanity was in perfect order.

When we're finally with Him, He'll do the same for us, completing the work He began when we were born: the decades-long disassembly of what's not perfect for that which is, including the final panel of that perfection—the redemption of our bodies (Romans 8:23). We will be like Him because we will see Him just as He is (1 John 3:2). It will be the great moment when "It is finished" is pronounced over us, too (John 19:30). The Spirit shares that promise through Paul with these words:

> For our citizenship is in heaven, from which also we eagerly wait for a Savior, the Lord Jesus Christ; who will transform the body of our humble state into conformity with the body of His glory, by the exertion of the power He has even to subject all things to Himself.
>
> PHILIPPIANS 3:20-21

Naomi (mentioned in chapter five) has a place in that life; so does Jeremiah, Daniel, Paul, and Job who, in the midst of profound loss and suffering, was inspired by the Spirit to say:

> As for me, I know my Redeemer lives, and at the last

He will take His stand on the earth. Even after my skin is destroyed, *yet from my flesh* I shall see God; whom I myself shall behold, and whom my eyes shall see and not another.

Job 19:25-27a (emphasis mine)

None of them knew full redemption here. Neither will we. All of them know it there. So will we; the full, eternal, depthless expression of Psalm 16:11, "You will make known to me the path of life; in Your presence is fullness of joy; in Your right hand there are pleasures forever." Everything related to the way we're made—everything susceptible to maiming, decay, or imperfection—will be restored fully, finally, and forever by the same Hand which wielded everything in the universe into existence. It will be so incomprehensible that descriptions of it germinated in well-intentioned but imperfect brains and genuflecting on screens and between book covers could never do it justice.

Not to worry. It's not necessary we do it justice.

He will, all in good time.

Chapter 14

NOW ABOUT THE
ELEPHANT IN THE ROOM

There are some people reading this book for whom the content is very likely a struggle. In fact, in a bad moment, the truths we've uncovered may serve to do nothing more than make tears flow. Ditto for those who love and care for them. Rather than bring hope and encouragement, the promise of a new body, free from imperfection and imbued with eternal youth, is a reminder of what they never had to start with—or what was taken from them through no fault of their own, an act of selfless bravery, or a moment of ignorance or foolishness which haunts them every single moment of every single day.

After all, it's one thing to talk about age dimming our eyesight or stealing our driver's license. That assumes one had them to start with. But what about those who don't know what the color blue looks like, how it feels to put their foot on an accelerator, haven't heard middle C in forty years, or who've only walked to the fridge for a snack in their dreams?

I'm talking about those among us who live day-in-and-day-out with a disability, people who would give anything to jog a hundred yard dash, play "Twinkle, Twinkle Little Star" on Grandma's old, out-of-tune piano, or slide store-bought cookie dough in the oven and punch up "10:00" on the timer. They're the ones for whom longings for the future are particularly acute and thus, potentially at least, very painful.

No doubt they look at otherwise healthy believers in Jesus Christ who mourn minor aches and pains and age-appropriate loss of whatever with a bit of disdain, thinking *if you only knew how fortunate you are to have had all that in the first place—and have some of it left.* Twenty or thirty years waiting for agelessness to arrive while still able to walk on the beach, dance with a spouse, or drive to the store for pain reliever is one thing. It's quite another to wait an entire lifetime, denied the physical abilities and pleasures which make the lull bearable.

It is calloused to encourage those who live in that world to "hang in there because eighty years from now, it won't make any difference." In my days as a pastor, I heard "well-intentioned" people using that kind of knock-off spirituality to avoid others' pain. Pretending to comfort, it is in reality an act of cowardice, a way to *appear* spiritual (there's that image-management thing again) while sidestepping the Spirit's instruction to "weep with those who weep" and "bear one another's burdens" (Romans 12:15, Galatians 6:2). I want to avoid that at all costs here.

Thus, allow me a moment to bring truth to light I trust God will use to support you and those who love you as you teeter on the balance point between ultimate, eternal perfection and immediate, temporal brokenness.

First, it's OK to struggle with moments of debilitating depression, wondering why in the name of all that's holy God brought a disability your way. You're not able to do what others can and you hate it. You feel cheated. How can a God who claims the surnames "Love" and "Grace" possibly justify wrapping your life in a suffocating blanket of diminished capacity? What kind of Being puts people in this world and doesn't allow them the pleasures and abilities others have—and destines those so debilitated with a lifetime of watching others do and enjoy what they can't?

I wouldn't think of disrespecting you by coughing up an empty, self-protective answer. The truth is, I don't have an answer. No one does.

But I can tell you God gives you permission to sling the questions, confusion, and depression His way. Though it's never correct to assault His character—that is, to call Him a liar, cheat, fraud or anything else derogatory—it is entirely appropriate and thoroughly biblical to cry out to Him with paralyzing doubt, deep-seated confusion, and profound discouragement.

The Psalms are chili-peppered with examples. For starters, read Psalms 44 and 88. Then there is: "Why do You stand afar off, O Lord? Why do you hide Yourself in times of trouble?" (Psalm 10:1) and "How long, O Lord? Will You forget me forever? How long will You hide Your face from me?" (Psalm 13:1).

Psalm 22:1-2 chimes in with "My God, My God, why have you forsaken me?... O my God, I cry by day but You do not answer; and by night but I have no rest," as does Psalm 74:1, "O God, why have You rejected us forever? Why does Your anger smoke against the sheep of Your pasture?" Psalm 77:7-10 caps it all off with:

> Will the Lord reject forever? And will He never be favorable again? Has His lovingkindness ceased forever? Has His promise come to an end forever? Has

God forgotten to be gracious, or has He in anger with-
drawn His compassion? Selah. Then I said, "It is my
grief, that the right hand of the Most High has changed."

Notice something: The psalmists say things which *seem* true
but aren't. Does God stand aloof from us—or worse yet, proac-
tively *hide* from us forever? Can He forget? Does He ever forsake
His people (that is, abandon us with no hope of remedy now or
later)? Does He reject us for eternity? Does His lovingkindness
toward us stop—for all time?

In every case, the answer is no; yet God never rebukes psalmists for voicing how they felt. He wants us to be *that* candid
with Him. He wants us to know when we hurt, He's more interested in honesty than theological accuracy. He knows if we hang
in there with Him, the latter will come in due time. But if the
former doesn't precede it, the close-knit bond He desires with
us—when honesty in adversity gives way to trust—will never
come about.

Please don't subscribe to the notion crying out to Him must
be laden with high-church language and sanctified procedure.
Just *tell* Him. Don't tell Him the way someone else tells you to
tell Him. Tell Him the way *you'd* tell Him. He *made you* so He
wants to hear *from* you *about* you.

You may be afraid you'll say something wrong or out of His
will. Forget that mess. Trust God the Spirit to work with God the
Son to craft the imperfection in your prayer into something the
Father is anxious to hear (Isaiah 30:18, Romans 8:26-27, Hebrews
7:25). It's what the psalmists did—and He never reprimanded
them for moments when pain blocked their view of His character.

You're in good company when you do. Jesus Christ recited Psalm
22:1 on the Cross (Matthew 27:46). Don't let anyone convince

you that as God, He knew the Father's abandonment was coming so it was easier.

Rubbish. Hebrews 5:7 is clear there were lessons about being human He could only learn through suffering—more horrible than any of us will ever know. As gut-wrenching as some of our experiences are, we've never borne the weight of the world's sin and suffered total punishment and abject separation from God the Father for it. I'm convinced it was His greatest moment of torment. If He felt the freedom to cry out to His Father in that kind of anguish, how much more should we in our hopelessness, doubt, and pain?

Second, remember Jesus Christ knows what it's like to be disabled—because He was. How else would we describe torn flesh, ravaged musculature, bones out of joint, disfigurement, slow suffocation, burning thirst, and indescribable pain? True, His lasted hours not decades, and it did not require the routine challenges to personal care and hygiene some endure. But do not think for a moment You have someone at Your side who does not know what it means to have your body go south on you. He does—and as we pointed out earlier in the book, His intellectual, emotional, and spiritual memory is perfect. He knows exactly what it feels like and precisely how to help you (Hebrews 2:17-18, 4:14-16).

But there's a problem. We don't want His help to be the ability to continue living with what we have, do we? We want pain and struggle to disappear immediately, if not sooner. We want Him to sweep in like a Holy Commando and blow it all to kingdom come. That, we reason, would be a far greater testimony to His love, grace, and power than allowing us to wallow in difficulty. After all, disabled Christians are just another excuse for the world to mock God for being so "loving."

God may have a miracle in store for you here, in this life. He is, after all, the God of all flesh; there is nothing too difficult for Him and He has more than demonstrated His ability to heal (Jeremiah 32:27, Luke 5:17-26, 7:1-10, Acts 3:1-10). However, it's more likely you will be called on to continue facing physical, mental, and emotional challenges—and the battleships of despair the enemy sails into your life because of them—for reasons you may not fully understand.

But hear God clearly on this. It is NOT due to your lack of faith.

I realize there are some who might argue otherwise, convinced if you just believed more, you could walk out of the house holding your mat like the paralytic in Luke 5:17-26. Is that so? I guess that's why Jesus left Capernaum without healing everyone. The only people left were wretches schlepping false faith, fighting for morsels of power trailing off His robe as He rolled out of town (Mark 1:33-39).

If that's the way He operates, why didn't He ask for character references before miraculously feeding five thousand men (plus women and children, see Matthew 14:15-21)? Surely there were some sin-infested, ne'er-do-wells in that crowd. Why didn't He vet the man with the withered hand (Mark 3:1-5)?

Are we to believe Paul told Timothy to drink wine for his stomach problems and frequent ailments because Timothy lacked enough faith for a miracle (1 Timothy 5:23)? Really? Paul left a man of anemic faith in Ephesus to establish and strengthen the church? And what of Paul? He described His disability as a "thorn in the flesh." He begged God on three occasions to take it away. He never did. Was a lack of faith the culprit—or did God have something else in mind (2 Corinthians 12:1-10)?

Which leads to a final point: *Take heart the effect and power of your life are not bound by your physical limitations.* You may not be able to swim laps, ride a bike, spiral a football, stitch a quilt, or stride up a staircase. Quadratic equations and the Heisenberg principle may be beyond your grasp. But remember one of the major themes of this book is Jesus Christ has never, isn't, and never will be limited by our imperfections. All of us must count on Him to do things we cannot do for ourselves, among them forgiveness and justification, Spirit-driven enablement for each day, and, at the end of life, the transformation of these animated cadavers we call bodies into something far greater than we've ever known.

Be careful, though. His promise to display power in your weakness does not mean you will do "great things for God" as we typically define it. The Bible never uses that phrase to describe a life of faith. You will probably never be on a local news "Inspiring Stories" segment, have a building named in your honor, or hear national sports figures or network reporters highlighting your life as one which stirs others to reach for the stars (whatever that means).

A life of significance, beauty, and meaning—one which creates excited whispers in the halls of heaven—courageously accepts that obscurity impaired with weakness, inability, and setback is where God often does His best work. Our task is to accept what we've been given, be faithful in the thousands of mundane, seemingly insignificant things which comprise most of our days, and trust He'll use our crumpets of (dis)ability to do what only He can.

The effect may be vast and noticeable or small and barely discernible. It does not matter. He will have done what is in His best interest—the one and only measure of "great things." You will have been His partner, something He cherishes more than you know. And when the day of your departure arrives, the day when your doubts are quenched and questions silenced, when you gaze at the beauty of heaven like Curtis Lashley did,[14] there will be only one thing left for *Him* to say and *you* to do: "Stand up, My partner and friend. It's time to toss that wheelchair in the air like a mortarboard. Be whole. Be complete. Be *you*. Your Graduation Day has come."

---

14. Curtis was the Lyon family doctor and friend you met in chapter one.

Chapter 15

WHEN NUTHIN' DOIN'
IS ALL WE'VE GOT

L ife has taught me most Christians—people who've come to grips with the totality of their sin and believe the only One who can save them from its eternal penalty is Jesus Christ (God in the flesh); and He provided that salvation through His crucifixion, death, burial, and resurrection—people like that are confused about life's purpose.

It's easy to understand why. We're barraged with messages we're here to find our passion, pursue our dreams, and work hard to accomplish whatever we put our hearts to. In other words, the secret to life is giving the world a bigger carbon footprint of Me.

That doesn't just come from the secular world. Some in the church magnify it, too—personal achievement with some Jesus sprinkled on top. They believe Christianity's true mark of authenticity is good deeds done by self-declared good people to impress and persuade Him we're worth loving—or to dazzle others. It's about us looking good.

You may object it's not about us but Him—and you'd be correct.

But listen carefully to some sermons and other Christian messaging today and you'll hear a troubling undercurrent of self-actualized achievement or self-determined purpose intent on showing others what *we're* like.

I'm here to tell you that's as bankrupt as the day is long.

Please understand. I am not saying good works are wrong or unnecessary. Passages like Proverbs 31:8-9, Matthew 5:16, John 15:1-8, Ephesians 2:10, 1 Timothy 2:9-10, 5:9-10, 6:18, 2 Timothy 3:16-17, and Titus 2:7-8 are clear we've been created for good works designed to bring glory to our heavenly Father—that is, to show others what *He's* like.

I'm saying many have lost sight of *that* purpose. We've turned displays of His character into placards of personal or congregational virtue. How many times have you heard someone—Christian or non-Christian—say performing some altruistic service made them feel good about themselves?

That should tell us something. It's a tip off our motivation is out of whack, that it's not about the child who needs a mentor or the shut-in who needs a touch of God's grace through a meal and a few minutes of companionship. It's about us and what makes us think of ourselves as we want to think; that we are good and God and other people are impressed.

There's an ancient phrase for that, one we first encountered in chapters six and seven. It's called "being a Pharisee." As we learned there, self-righteousness is like tying a three-quarter inch cotton rope to a one hundred ton boxcar and pulling it up Pike's Peak. Some of us recognize that as a foundational truth of the Bible. "For by grace you have been saved through faith," the Holy Spirit said through Paul, "and that not of yourselves, it is the gift of God; *not as a result of works* so that no one may boast" (Ephesians 2:8-9, emphasis mine. See Psalm 49:5-9 and 2 Timothy 1:9 also).

Sadly, the Pharisees and other religious elites never got it. They went 'all in' on hijacking the Mosaic Law as the way to get to heaven on their own, completely blind to its role as a tutor to lead them to Christ (John 5:39-40, Galatians 4:21-26).

It's easy to gaze over 2,000 years of church history and wonder how they missed it. Yet many Christians today do the same thing. Having started with the helpless faith which drove us to Christ in the first place, we've continued our spiritual journey believing works now fuel our relationship with Him.

We touched on this in chapter seven. It bears repeating here. Again, note the Spirit's words through the apostle Paul, the former Pharisee:

> This is the only thing I want to find out from you: did you receive the Spirit by the works of the Law, or by hearing with faith? Are you so foolish? Having begun by the Spirit, are you now being perfected by the flesh? Did you suffer so many things in vain—if indeed it was in vain? So then, does He who provides you with the Spirit and works miracles among you, do it by the works of the Law, or by hearing with faith?
>
> GALATIANS 3:2-5

We met Jesus' friend Martha in chapter twelve. One day, she and her sister, Mary, invited Him to their home for a meal. At first glance, it would seem Mary was negligent and uncaring in not assisting Martha in her dinner preparations. After all, He was *the LORD*. He deserved the very best.

Instead, Mary chose to sit at His feet and get to know Him. Martha protested He didn't seem to care she'd been left to *do all the work alone* and told Him to tell her to lend a hand. His response? "Martha, Martha, you are anxious and troubled about many things; but one thing is necessary. Mary has chosen the good portion, which will not be taken away from her" (Luke 10:41-42, ESV).

Like Martha, too many of us believe the helpless faith which brought us *to* Him is insufficient to sustain life *with* Him. We've been convinced "weakness and the inability to do anything without Him" makes a nice refrigerator magnet—but that's it. So we power our relationship forward with works, convinced He'll only be impressed if we blow an engine trying to please Him.

Yet Jesus Christ never intended us to carry the burden of a life of faith by ourselves. He knows we can't. As mentioned earlier in the book, He is driven to do things for us we cannot do for ourselves. We began with Him that way and He wants us to live with Him that way (John 15:5, 2 Corinthians 12:9-10).

It's also His intention we die with Him that way.

En route to our eternal youthfulness, some of us will linger at death's door for what may seem an eternity. If we have built our lives on doing *for* Him, what happens when we no longer can? Will life have meaning and value—or will our final days mean the rusted hull of our purpose and worth is dry docked for good?

If we know better—and we should—we'll take heart being moored in inactivity is just as significant as being under full sail in the open water of accomplishment. That's because the secret to a life of faith, a life He is pleased with, is a commitment to *know Him so we can learn to trust Him.* All *that* requires is faith and a heartbeat; which means a hospital room or hospice gurney is just as holy and meaningful as a soup kitchen or the medical mission field. Mary, after all, was just *sitting.*

Years ago a friend told me when his grandmother was in her last days, about all she could do was sit in a chair. Daily productivity for her family, friends, church, and anyone else God brought her way was all but gone. For her, the days were literally, nuthin' doin.'

When visitors came, she asked them to read her the Bible. The minute their voice carried His Words to her ears, she'd steel herself against both arms of her chair, sit up as straight as she could, and look intently at the reader. Her body waned; her heart could not. Her Lord was speaking to her. They could still spend time together. She could still fulfill her purpose.

That story stirs me and I hope stirs you to know if we're in a similar situation one day, we can follow her lead. All these years later, what we learned in chapter eleven holds true: God faithfully dispenses grace on her behalf to those of us left behind. Through her, He reminds us life's most enduring purpose is the journey from hearing about God to truly understanding Him. That is, to discover what He's *actually* like and how much He loves us so we can rest in His Spirit as He shepherds us through His Word and this life (Job 42:5).

That sweet, powerful soul—a lion of faith temporarily dressed in the tear-away jersey of an old woman—never lost sight of that. She knew the days leading to her death were her final way to spend time with Him—and thus glorify Him (John 21:19). Not through works. He's done the work. Through knowledge. Through faith and trust embroidered on the arms of a chair. She chose the good portion and it was not taken away from her.

Now she's with Him. So's your grandmother who died of Alzheimer's, your dad of a heart attack, your uncle of a stroke, your brother from a motorcycle accident, your daughter, niece, cousin, sister, mom and granddaughter who were escorted home by cancer. They're enjoying life with The One Who gave it—not in infirmity but perfection, not in old age or debilitated mind, body, or spirit but alive in an explosive youthfulness full of activity with Him and for Him that knows no end. Their works didn't get them there. His did. As we've discovered, right now, at this moment, whether you realize it, feel it, or even understand it, He's preparing you for that life, too. It's what He's been about since you were conceived. The Holy Spirit assures us of it through the prophet Isaiah, who gave God's people in the OT a promise just as valid for us:

> Listen to Me, O house of Jacob, and all the remnant of the house of Israel, you who have been borne by Me from birth and have been carried from the womb; even to your old age I will be the same, and even to your graying years I will bear you! I have done it, and I will carry you; and I will bear you and I will deliver you.

> ISAIAH 46:3-4

It doesn't matter you can no longer run the forty-yard dash in 4.4, play "Orange Blossom Special" like a madman or bake blue-ribbon cakes. As we've seen, His promise is not predicated on your physical or mental condition. He is the same yesterday, today, and forever (Hebrews 13:8). There is no variation or change of heart with Him. What He says He will do, He will do (Isaiah 46:10, 55:11, James 1:17). Which means one day, 4.4 will stand for the milliseconds it takes you to run the forty and you'll play "Orange Blossom Special" like a madman *while* baking cakes.

The prophet Malachi's prediction of our future is worth a final moment: "But for you who fear My name, the sun of righteousness will rise with healing in its wings; and you will go forth and skip about like calves from the stall" (Malachi 4:2). Does that sound like someone with MS or a congenital heart condition?

How about quadriplegia, Parkinson's, glaucoma, or COPD? Yes, we will carry our infirmities and imperfections to the grave—but no further. There is no room for physical imperfection in a world dominated by Jesus Christ. That's impossible. Everything defective and disabled will be Deep Sixed in His glory. Every capability we possess—whether we use them every day or they've been dormant for decades—will reach its zenith in that world—ours to enjoy and His to glory in.

I assure you there's no epitaph in the world like that.

Chapter 16

ONE DAY AT THE BEACH

I couldn't believe how good I felt.

I'd had runner's high before but this was like nothing I'd known. Air moved through my lungs in a way I thought only world-class athletes experienced. My body was in perfect cadence—arms, chest, and torso riding the backbeat of legs beating a rhythm steady as a metronome, my bare feet effortlessly tossing patches of sand in the air like confetti.

The scenery was breathtaking. Sand whiter than I thought possible stretched ahead in a broadband of silicon dioxide without one ripple of imperfection. Nuanced textures were perfect; every grain of quartz seemed to know it's place. Luxurious fairways more perfect than any golf course I'd ever seen chaperoned the beach toward the horizon. Trees painted in variegated greens, some I'd never seen, swayed gently in a breeze more refreshing than I've ever felt. Beyond them cliffs with beveled faces so beautiful they looked as if only the Lord Himself could have chiseled them, rose just high enough to accentuate the beauty they guarded, but not so high as to transgress a zircon blue sky unfurled from heaven.

Gentle waves rolled in, calling my name. I ignored them for a while, not wanting to break off a great run. But after a few minutes I couldn't resist and broke for the surf. As soon as my feet hit the water, I launched into an arching dive which seemed to carry me seventy yards out over the water, and slipped beneath the surface with barely a splash. A few seconds later I broke the surface and rolled on my back, laughing and splashing like a six-year-old after his first body surf. The water was cleaner and more refreshing than I can describe.

I started to swim. The same meter and rhythm my body had known on the beach took over, this time with a stroke the greatest swimmers in history train for years to achieve. It was effortless. There was no breathlessness. No strain. I was moving through the water with what seemed like impossible speed. After a bit I stopped to get my bearings and realized I was almost a mile down the beach. I was stunned and honestly, a little disoriented. "How in the world could I ...?"

That's when I heard it—a voice with hints of familiarity but somehow different, too. It was noble and empowered, booming with strength yet as gentle as the breeze serenading the beach. I listened.

There it was again. This time, I honed in on its source. It was coming from someone on the beach, waving at me. "Be right there!" he said. He wasn't yelling. He didn't even cup his hands to his mouth. Yet his voice carried perfectly over what must have been three hundred yards. I could hear every word as if he were right next to me.

Old instincts would have whispered, "Stranger on the beach says he'll be right there. Sorry friend but this is where I exit, stage right." But that seemed misplaced in this place. All I felt was calm and peace, so I waited.

And watched.

He was coming with the same speed I'd felt moments before. I'd never seen a human being move through the water like that. And that stroke. I knew that stroke. Smooth as molasses. Perfect body roll with elbows high, spine as straight as a loblolly pine. He popped up right in front of me and realization met recognition. It was my Dad.

"Hey buddy!" he said, "How are you?"

The last time I saw him, he was bedridden in a hospice facility in Scottsdale, Arizona, clinging to life while Alzheimer's completed its work. I wasn't there when he left earth. I'd returned home to Chicago four days before and just finished dinner with my life-long friend and college roommate when my Mom called to let me know he was gone. I'd spoken with him a few hours earlier, via a phone my brother held to his ear so I could tell him good-bye. I told him how proud I was to be his son, that he'd been a wonderful father, and I was grateful he was about to see and hear things far greater than anything he'd experienced in this world.

Was I sad to say goodbye? Of course. Despite the demands of owning an advertising agency when I was a boy, he found time to throw a football with me in the backyard, take the family on camping trips across the United States, and pop for tickets to ball games. When it was time for me to fly the coop, he and my Mom foot the bill for college (with a little help from my summer jobs) and loved me enough to let me cut my own path in life with their undying support.

Now there would be no more memories to create; no more backpacking in the Grand Canyon or riotous laughter over the twisted face of his eight-month-old granddaughter tasting lemon yogurt for the first time. I wouldn't hear his home-spun wisdom advising caution against taking wooden nickels, that a snug fit is tight as Dick's hatband, or his commentary a desolate landscape is just land holding the world together. His time was done. Our time was done. What began with him cradling me in his arms, spoon-feeding Gerber's to his first born, ended with me cradling a phone, spoon-feeding him love and respect from two thousand miles away. Like we said before, death stinks.

But the sadness and grief didn't matter now. It was information without impact, facts with no need for feelings, yesterday's news from a world neither he nor I had any inkling to pay attention to. That was then. Then was gone. This was now. Now is forever.

I can't describe the look on his face. Every bit my father. Every bit the Lord. I'd seen pictures of him when he was young, of course. But this. This was different. Youth personified. Youth embellished with the perfection of Jesus Christ, who'd taken my dad's leftovers and made a feast of agelessness with it. He was perfectly himself, perfectly reflecting the Lord who created him in utero and recreated him here. Man, he looked great.

He'd always loved the water. He was on his college swim team, which is where that stroke made in heaven got its start. He loved taking me, my Mom, and my brother and sister to the beach. As a little boy, I used to stand at the water's edge and watch him play in the waves, wanting to be with him but too afraid of the mountain range of water churning between us.

One day, he decided it was time I join him. He took me in his arms and into the surf. I was OK for a while. But like Peter on another sea over 1,900 years before, I started concentrating on the waves more than the one holding me. I panicked. Tears cliff-dove off my cheeks to splash around with their salt-water kin.

I begged him to take me back to the safe, soft sand and the comfort of my Mother's hand. He tried to reassure me he had me, that there was nothing to be afraid of, but the waves sounded louder and more powerful than he was. After a few failed attempts to convince me the danger was nothing to fear, he obliged.

Now here we were, playing out the same scene, a moment orchestrated by The One in whom all things, in all ways, are summed up, redeemed, and made perfect—even a father and son moment at the beach. I was with my Dad in the waves. And I wasn't afraid anymore.

We took off together for the shore, hitching a ride on two manta rays "just happening" by. Once there, we ran through the trees and started up one of the cliffs that seemed engraved just for us. A trek that would have taken hours in the other world took just a few minutes. When we reached the top, we stood in the glow of a world illumined by His light, so powerful you can actually *feel* it, marveling at sights and sounds beyond anything we'd known. The view was incredible. We could see Forever.

We ran down the back side of the cliffs like schoolboys romping down a hillside. Back on the beach, we fell in stride with each other, running effortlessly, side-by-side. I remembered another moment, from the world before, running next to him at the gym. He was wearing a T-shirt I'd given him with "I may be slow… but I'm ahead o' you" written on the back. (He thought it was as funny as I did). I was young and nimble. He was middle-aged and a bit stiff, working hard to keep pace.

Not anymore. Age differences were a thing of the past. There was no age. There was no difference. We were as He'd intended from the Beginning. The pace was fluid and powerful. The setting seemed even more beautiful than when I dove in the water a few… minutes? hours? before. I couldn't tell. It didn't matter. Time doesn't just stand still in this place. It leaves the building.

Soon, we heard other footsteps, coming from everywhere, joining in the cadence. Family. Friends. The auto shop manager. The ex-Navy SEAL. High school chums and college roommates. The nurse at the oncologist's. Faces from the past who, by the Spirit's power, had vaulted dialysis machines and infusion centers, battlefields, hospice gurneys, cemeteries, and mausoleums to stick the mother of all landings in the place "whose architect and builder is God" (Hebrews 11:10). The greetings we had with each other ... I cannot tell you what it was like. We were in the place where joy and happiness join hands and throw their arms in the air in victory. There are no words.

We laughed and joked. My cousin, the outside-the-box childhood rascal turned by-the-book accountant, swiped his childhood back and did the moonwalk. We fell out all over the beach. Funniest thing I've ever seen. We howled for who knows how long. Then we leaped to our feet like twenty-somethings body-snatched by five-year-olds and continued on our way. It was unbelievable. The unity, the joy, the sense of wonder ... it was outta this world. Literally. I didn't think it could get any better.

But it did.

We all felt it, all at once. The Power. The Love. We first experienced it when the Spirit effortlessly uncoupled us from our bodies and powered us through the heavens toward home. We'd been living in its glow ever since. But now there was a special pulse of it, behind us, chasing us down. We stopped and turned. Everyone, all at once. (That happens a lot here, by the way. The unity of the Spirit in the bond of peace, Ephesians 4:3).

It was Him.

He'd split that zircon-blue sky open like a theatre curtain and was sweeping down toward us, arms outstretched, nail-imprinted palms turned our way. Don't ask me how, but every one of us saw our names written in those wounds—not marks of imperfection but a memorial to the perfect healing He'd given us (Isaiah 53:5,

1 Peter 2:24). When His feet hit the water, angels sprang from the spray, shouting His name. We shouted it back. He skimmed along its surface, smiling and laughing like a Big Brother rushing the court 'cause little bro' just scored the game-winning basket. He asked if He could crash the party—and we went crazy.

Think of the most explosively joyous moment you've ever had: in the middle of eighty-thousand fans screaming their lungs out at a last minute, championship-winning touchdown—or busting through the delivery room doors with your hands in the air to let everyone know your first born was here. Now put a multiplier on it, something akin to a "1" with ten or twenty zeroes. Not even close.

What we felt was indescribable; joyous sounds and emotions which shot past chaos and sin and landed between perfection and flawlessness. Someone broke into a new song for Him, their voice thundering with gentleness and shimmering like a crystal waterfall. The melody was completely unique and totally familiar. After one time through, we joined in with harmonies and counterpoint which would have taken the old world's best choirs days to perfect. We were smiling. He was smiling right back—at each of us individually and all of us collectively—all at once. I have no idea how He does that. But He does it all the time. All things, in all ways ...

We finished and crowded around Him, laughing with delight like children when Dad comes home from work. The look of absolute joy on His face was, well ... I'm wordless again.

We built a fire on the beach. Actually, we gathered the wood and He spoke the flame into existence. We shared collective stories and individual vignettes of His power and faithfulness, conversing with no pretense, no manipulation, no errors or half-truths, no embellishments or dysfunction to make the story or ourselves better than we are. There is no need for that here. We value and love each other perfectly because we are perfectly loved, making us perfectly justified, perfectly satisfied, perfectly at peace with Him and each other. Every hurt and injustice erased; every relationship healed. To put it another way, we had the joy of youth (with none of its insecurity) and all the wisdom of the Spirit. It was a scene we'd hoped for a million times in the other world. Now it was ours with no end.

Angels suddenly appeared and served us a meal like you can't imagine, custom-made for each of us, cooked to perfection, just the way we like. It was like they read our minds and knew exactly what we were craving. He spent time with each of us—never in a hurry, never looking around like He wanted to "get this over with so He could go over there and talk to them." Trust me, you haven't had a conversation until you've had one with Jesus Christ looking right at you, totally engaged, making you feel like there's no one else in the universe He'd rather talk with than you.

There was no shame in the interchange; no looking down at the sand and kicking it with our feet for fear of looking Him in the Eye. There was no judgment in His face. There is no judgment in This Place. Only Love. After all, this is where faith and hope are spoken of in the past tense. They've done their job. Here, there is only Love. For Good. And Forever.

I thought of sin. Not the acts. I couldn't remember the acts. Not one single thing I'd ever done. I knew I had. I just couldn't remember the details. And I certainly couldn't remember what it *felt* like to sin—or the hurt and anger of sins committed against me (the benefit of having the mind of Christ). Like everything else in the former world, when I "died" there, so did my sin. Everyone's did. Completely. Every act and memory flicked out of heaven like a bread crumb.

Instead I thought of sin, the fact. That is, humanity mired in the swamp of disobedience, oblivious to sin's incursion in the Garden yielding the forfeiture of this scene, heaven on earth, which He'd enjoyed with Adam and Eve and wanted desperately to have with them—and us—again.

I thought of what it took for Him to get it back, that He voluntarily broke His body so mine could be restored, serving up compassion, grace, patience, and loyal, committed love on the altar of truth and justice—the truth of our sin and rebellion and the justice required to quell it's fury. I realized this scene was on His mind when He hung there, knowing this moment depended on that moment, when the Man in Him personified the greatest weakness so the God in Him could display the greatest strength. The looks on *our faces* now made Him "set *His face* to go to Jerusalem" to accomplish what we never could (Luke 9:51, ESV). It's what He always wanted. It's what He always wanted for us.

Now we were with Him, enjoying every eternal moment of it; and He was with us—enjoying it even more. Finally, His kingdom was what it was before: The place where eternally youthful love lives, born of the Father's heart, wielded by the Savior's hand(s), and nurtured by the Spirit's leading. Souls stained by sin and bodies worn out by imperfection have no place here. It can only be enjoyed by those perfectly designed to accommodate His glory: *You* and *me*—flawless expressions of what He made you and me to be.

That's why I can say to you fear not, friends. The imperfection we wear now is a temporary garment whose purpose is to prepare us for the youthfulness He waits to drape us in when He shepherds us through time and space to the other side. It's the place where "age" is only spoken of in the plural, as in the *ages* to come in which the surpassing riches of His grace in kindness are waiting (Ephesians 2:7).

The only thing to do now is trust Him to use aging as a tool to get us ready, confident what appears and feels so real now is, as we've said, life's greatest illusion. Just as His suffering and death veiled the reality awaiting Him, ours does the same. It hurts now, yes. Age robs us of what we once had, something we thought was ours to keep, our birthright in a broken world. But we wouldn't want eternal youthfulness here, anyway. It would just propel us through one agonizing eon after another, doomed to live with a hint of perfection but never able to grasp it.

He would never do that to us. Agelessness *is* our eternal birthright, the one He gave Adam and Eve in the Garden and secured for all their descendants when He mutilated sin on the Cross and broke it's seal on His tomb. But it is designed to be lived in a perfect world, the antithesis of every imperfection we see here, so it's full benefits can be fully maximized.

That's why anyone whose faith rests in Him can say with the fullest assurance possible there aren't any old people in heaven. There can't be. He won't permit it. What's happening to us now—broken hips and blood thinners, breast cancer and bipolar disorder, hearing aids, hepatitis, ALS and lupus—all of it—is simply a reminder our faith in Him and His promises means aging, illness, and death aren't robbing of us anything. They're a testimonial we're about to gain everything, that the moment we "lay aside our earthly dwelling" is at hand (2 Peter 1:14)—and ultimate physical, emotional, mental, and spiritual salvation is about to take hold. As we've said all along, it means we're not getting old.

We're getting ready.

The Lord will accomplish what concerns me;
Your lovingkindness, O Lord, is everlasting,
Do not forsake the works of Your Hands

PSALM 138:8

Chapter 17

CAREFUL. DON'T BURN YOURSELF

If you were like me growing up, your parents had "good" rules you didn't much care for: no snacks before dinner, a bath every night (at least in the summer), coming to meals on time and asking to be excused when finished, no TV on school nights (though come to think of it, that may have been a Lyon-family special), addressing elders as "Sir" and Ma'am," and no ugly words or name calling.

But I doubt you had much of a problem with what you probably heard if you got too close to a campfire: "Careful. Don't burn yourself." Sure, it was fun to sit close enough to turn a stick into a sparkler, roast marshmallows, or scorch a hot dog. But earlobes turning to griddle cakes or smoke coming off the bottom of your sneakers was enough to realize Mom and Dad knew what they were talking about.

Jesus Christ has his own version of that warning—given for humanity's good but tragically, too often dismissed or ignored. We find it in Luke 16:19-31, where he describes two men—a nameless rich man who "habitually dressed in purple and fine linen, joyously living in splendor every day; and a poor man named Lazarus [who] was laid at his gate, covered with sores, longing to be fed with the crumbs falling from the rich man's table" (vv. 19-21). Lazarus' condition was so miserable it included dogs licking his sores.

Death came calling. Lazarus was taken to heaven; the rich man to Hades (hell). Jesus tells us he was in torment and looked into heaven to see Lazarus enjoying comfort with Abraham (the father of justification by faith, not works). He begged Abraham to send Lazarus to dip the tip of his finger in water and cool off his tongue because "I am in agony in this flame" (v. 24). Please note he had a body and experienced physical pain, thirst, and enormous emotional torment.

He was told he'd had his turn at the good things—and Lazarus at the bad—and it was time for the roles to reverse. In addition, there was a "great chasm" between them "so those who wish to come over from here to you will not be able, and none may cross over from there to us" (v. 26).

In other words, the rich man's fate was sealed. Again, please note there is no mention of a release date or parole for good behavior. He was there for (nothing) good. His entire life, He'd wanted God out of the picture. Now He was.

Before his voice fell silent everywhere but hell, he offered one last plea, begging Abraham to send Lazarus to his five living brothers to warn them so they could avoid joining him in torment. He was told they have the writings of Moses and the prophets and they should listen to them. He objected, convinced if someone went to them from the dead, "they will repent" (vv. 27-30). The response is chilling: "If they do not listen to Moses and the

Prophets, they will not be persuaded even if someone rises from the dead" (v. 31).

That makes the question pretty simple.

Are you listening?

There are excuses not to: "The Bible has errors and I don't trust it," "Any God who would send people to hell isn't loving and I want nothing to do with Him" or "I don't believe God sends anyone to hell." Okay. I get it. But allow me to ask if your objections are more about avoiding an inconvenient truth than fact-based, well-reasoned conviction. Read Psalm 19:7-11, which describes the perfection of God's Word; 2 Timothy 3:16-17, which says the Bible is inspired (literally, "God-breathed"); and 2 Peter 1:20-21 which says no biblical prophecy is an act of human interpretation or will, "but men moved by the Holy Spirit spoke from God." If God is Who He says, those passages mean He's not only capable of communicating His truth; He has. Which means Luke 16 is true.

If God isn't loving, how do we explain Jesus Christ's willingness to die for mankind's sin including those who brutalized him physically and hurled verbal abuse at Him as He hung on the Cross (Matthew 27:39-44, Mark 10:45, 15:16-20, Luke 23:13-39, John 3:16, 5:24, Romans 5:6-11)? Reject that, and we're telling Christ He doesn't know what He's talking about; that His suffering to counterbalance the horror of hell for all who believe is the deranged self-expression of the most self-consumed lunatic in human history. Okay. How do we know that? Who of us has gone to heaven, interviewed God, and found out the man claiming to be His "Son" is a fraud?

We can object there's just too much pain and suffering in the world to believe in a loving God, but what about the responsibility we bear for how messed up things are? God doesn't pollute oceans, lie, murder, steal, cheat, bribe, or pervert justice. He doesn't abort babies, sell drugs on the street, extort, run Ponzi schemes, or blame others when we're wrong. *We* do those things. Shouldn't we be held responsible?

The classic objection is He could stop us; and since He hasn't He's either non-existent, incompetent, or apathetic. Yet that ignores the clear promise that one day He will (Isaiah 65:17, 66:22, 2 Peter 3:10-13, Revelation 20:11-15). Every wrong will be made right. Every injustice will be dealt with. Every sin against Him and crime against humanity will be punished. He's delaying that judgment so as many as possible can find forgiveness, peace, and eternal life (Psalm 2, Romans 9:22-23, 1 Timothy 2:3-4, 2 Peter 3:9). It is sobering to realize if He brought an end to this age five minutes from now and you still didn't believe in Him, you and the rich man would be neighbors. Well, not neighbors. There is nothing neighborly about hell. Sinful human beings in pain hurt each other. That's what you'd have. Is that what you want (Daniel 12:2)?

Consider this, too. At this point in history, He's chosen to let us operate with free will, which means we're free to pollute, pervert, lie, steal, kill, maim, and destroy. If He forced us to stop without changing our nature, He'd be the most brutal dictator in history. As we learned in chapter seven, His justice would require punishment for our actions *and* thoughts, meaning we'd all be in labor camps or before a firing squad. Instead, He chose to lay all that guilt on His Son, punish Him, and offer us the chance to escape His coming judgment. That's not ineptitude or lack of concern. It's Patience and Grace beyond measure (again, see Romans 9:22-23).

Think of it this way: It's *good* to teach children to do *good*—and to invoke negative consequences when they don't. It's *good* when our judicial system tries and incarcerates the guilty. It's *good* when people square up, admit fault, and receive forgiveness. Yet we say it's *not good* if God operates the same way. Sorry, but I have to stick up for my Savior. That's just not fair. We can't have it both ways. We can't call things good when we do them but not good when He does. Life doesn't work like that. Neither does eternity.

Finally, if God truly doesn't send anyone to hell, then why does it upset us if some claim He does? They'll just be proven wrong in the end, right? No big deal. All's well that ends well. No harm, no foul. If it does upset us, isn't it possible it's because we fear it might be true and it's just too hard to face? It's like refusing to go to the doctor when we notice a lump under our arm: If we don't have a diagnosis, we don't have cancer. It's irrational, completely untethered from reality, and may cost us our life—but it's the way we are. Not good.

<hr />

All of this to say, the end of this life could put you on another beach, where the white strands of perfection, joy, and peace have given way to the molten sands of human choice, sin, and judgment. There are no zircon blue skies guarded by cliffs chiseled with the artistry of the Great Hand. There is nowhere to play and laugh and look upon an eternal future with everlasting joy, where faith and hope are no longer necessary because they've been eclipsed with unending Love.

There will be no Savior bearing your name on His palms. Instead, His wounds will contain the indictment of your sin which inflicted injuries on Him for which you must now pay the price. The One Who could have been your Savior will be your Prosecutor. That will not go well (Romans 2:12-16, Revelation 20:11-15).

There will be no angelic shouts of praise to which you can add your voice because it will be forever parched with the thirst of regret, raw with anxiety and anguish from knowing there is no escape. No meals served by angels commissioned to serve you forever; only the delicacies of chaos and hate made possible by demonic beings who lied to you in this world so you'd suffer a fate worse than death in the next.

You will have a body; not exploding with youthfulness and the inability to know hurt, injury, pain, sickness or death; not a source of eternal joy and thankfulness as you see and physically experience what He always intended. On the contrary, you will know only what's left: Pain. Sorrow. Disability. That is, sin's attendant circumstance in the old world but now its eternal substance, where the only aroma is the overwhelming stench of death—everywhere, all the time, all there is, nothing more. No pleasure in God—or from God. Forever.

In that moment—and the endless ones thereafter—you'll realize you, too, were getting old—and getting ready—but not for a world where the Light and Love of God permeates and sustains everything. You were getting ready for a world where the best was not to come, where youth once held is forever beyond your grasp, and the way you looked in your final days here—aged, inept, and over the hill—was just a preview of what awaits when you breathe the last life-giving air you'll ever know (Job 20:1-29, Isaiah 66:22-24).

Right now as you read this, people all over the globe are tumbling into that world, held in custody in bodies decimated with imperfection for a resurrection and trial which will confirm their guilt and send them back to the reality from which they came, proving once and for all where they've been since they died is the place justice demanded they be: Locked in sin. Locked away from Him (Matthew 10:28, Luke 16:19-31, John 5:28-29, Revelation 20:11-15). I beg you with everything I have, don't be one of them. There is time—here and now—to embrace the God Who loves you beyond measure, the One Who died and rose again to prove it, and Who wants to see you on His beach—with all of us—experiencing life in a perfect, youthful body the way it was meant to be lived.

His name is Jesus Christ. He is The One, True God—and wants to be your Savior, King, and Friend. He is the Greatest Person you could ever encounter, the boundless expression of nobility, courage, heart, strength, wisdom, love, joy, peace, patience, kindness, goodness, faithfulness, gentleness, and self-control. He wants to begin sharing all that with you now so anywhere, anytime, under any circumstances, you'll have SomeOne to bring your burdens to, confident He cares deeply for you (Psalm 55:22, 94:18-19, 1 Peter 5:7). And you'll have the joy of knowing one day, He'll reprise the symphony of His love for you—in body, soul, and spirit—in the Eternal Re-creation that awaits.

Please answer His call to lay the burden of your sin in His hands. He knows it's breaking you. You know it's breaking you. He wants to fix it. Let Him. Trust Him for the salvation you can never achieve on your own, accomplished for you through His life, death, and resurrection. You have nothing to lose but hell. Then walk with Him day-by-day in the promise of a new hope and life in which He ...

> *... redeems your life from the pit,*
> *crowns you with lovingkindness and compassion*

[and] satisfies your years with good things
so your youth is renewed like the eagle

PSALM 103:4-5

That, friend, is a promise worth dying for, one *He* died for, yours for the asking, no strings attached. He made you. He loves you. He wants you with Him. But He gave you a free will, one with which you can choose Him or reject Him. Choose Him. Choose Life. Eternal and Free. When you do, the Great Promise which starts when you place your faith in Him and stretches past the zircon sky will be yours to have and hold forever. Simply put, the Promise is Life like you've never known, one in which...

There are *no* old, imperfect people in heaven.

WHAT NOW?

If you're ready to lay hold of that promise, do this: One, find a Bible and review the following verses so you can be clear on what it means to believe in Jesus Christ. The New American Standard (NASB), The English Standard Version (ESV), the Holman Christian Standard Bible (HCSB), or the New King James Version (NKJV) are good choices because they are extremely accurate translations of the best biblical manuscripts.

    a. Jesus Christ is God-in-the flesh, created everything that exists, and has fully shown us what God is like (John 1:1, 14-18, 10:30-33, 14:9, Colossians 1:15-19, Hebrews 1:1-3).

    b. There's no way you can earn your way to heaven. No one is that good, all the time, which means without a Savior, your unforgiven sin destines you for hell when you die (1 Kings 8:46, Psalm 143:2, Ecclesiastes 7:20, Matthew 5:21-22, 5:48, 10:28, John 3:36, 5:24, Romans 3:20-23, Galatians 2:16-21, Revelation 20:11-15).

c. That means Jesus had to earn your right to go to heaven, which He willingly did out of His great love for you (Mark 10:45, John 3:16, 10:11-18, Romans 5:1-11). He accomplished it by living a perfect life (1 Peter 1:18-19, Hebrews 4:14-16, 7:26-28) which qualified Him to be the perfect sacrifice for all your past, present and future sins (Mark 10:45, Romans 6:10, Hebrews 10:12-14, 1 Peter 3:18). In the words of 2 Corinthians 5:21, "He (God the Father) made Him (Jesus Christ) who knew no sin to be sin on our behalf, so we might become the righteousness of God in Him." Faith in Who He Is and what He did for you means God will never condemn you to hell for your sins. It is His free, gracious gift to you (John 5:24, 10:27-30, Romans 3:21-26, 1 Timothy 1:12-17, Titus 3:5-7).

d. He rose from the dead three days after His crucifixion for your sins, proving He has conquered sin and eternal death. He is anxious to share that victory with you so you can have the promise of being with Him in heaven forever when you leave this earth. Placing your faith in Him secures that promise for you, which no power in heaven or hell can take away (Luke 24:1-12, John 5:24, 10:28-29, 14:1-3, Acts 2:22-24, 4:10-12, Romans 4:24-25, 1 Corinthians 15:1-8, Ephesians 2:4-10, Colossians 2:13-14).

Two, tell Him in your own words you believe what's listed above. (No need to repeat the verses. He already knows them). It doesn't have to be fancy, eloquent, or packed with false emotion. You don't need to use a single "thee" or "thou." It just needs to be a sincere expression of what you believe.

Three, read Luke 15:1-10. Every one of your sins—past, present, and future, no matter how horrible—are forgiven. You are cleansed. Permanently. As in, "forever." It is a declaration of His will, driven by His love for you. It does not—nor will it ever— depend on how you feel about yourself at any given moment. It also means *angels* are rejoicing. About you. Calling your name out in heaven. How cool is that? Let me be the first to welcome you home. You're family now. Part of *His* family. You're going to look *good* in that new body!

Four, find a church that faithfully teaches what the *Bible* says (not the latest news, trends and polls, or someone's opinion) and helps you understand how it applies to your life. It may take a few weeks or months. That's O.K. Ask Him to help you find one. He will. Once you do, attend every Sunday. Join a class or small group bible study to make new friends who will encourage and support you. And begin to serve in the church so you can have the joy of helping others with the skills the Holy Spirit gave you the moment you placed your faith in Christ (1 Corinthians 12:12-31, Ephesians 1:13-14, 4:7-16, Hebrews 10:24-25, 1 Peter 4:8-11).

Don't be surprised when you run into hypocrites. The greatest people on earth are in churches. So are some of phoniest. The Lord knows that. He'll deal with them in His time, His way. For your part, build friendships with people whose faith, while not perfect, is genuine and growing. Even some of them may disappoint you. Not to worry. Jesus Christ will never be unfaithful to you—and He is an expert at using imperfect people to develop

His perfect relationship with you and perfectly direct you toward His will for your life. Always remember the cornerstone of your faith is Him, not others, and the ultimate goal is knowing and serving *Him*.

Finally, expect Satan and his henchman to come after you. They can't take you to hell now so they'll make the only play they have left: shipwrecking your faith to neutralize your effectiveness for Christ. They are good at what they do. But when you trust Him in the attack, you'll find they are no match for Him.

What does that trust look like? One, it's fully confident the Lord will never allow a temptation to come your way for which there's not an escape (1 Corinthians 10:13). Two, it resists temptation by telling Satan, "The Lord rebuke you" knowing when you do, he has no choice but to turn tail and run (James 4:7, Jude 9). Three, it's knowing even when you stumble and sin, His forgiveness is always available (Psalm 32:1-5, 131:1-3, 1 John 1:9).

Four, it knows regardless of how chaotic or painful moments in your life may become, they are not powerful enough to block expressions of His love during those trials; and there is NO WAY God will fail in using those experiences to accomplish good in your life (that is, expressions of the Deep Six—His compassion, grace, patience, loyal love, truth and justice. See Romans 8:28, 31-39). Satan will tell you that's bunk, that hardship and pain means He either doesn't exist or doesn't love you. But He's a liar (John 8:44)—and he didn't give his life for you.

Trust The One Who did.

Epilogue

A MOMENT TO SAY, "THANKS"

As is the case with many things in life, God has been at work in me a long time to get this book ready for you. Years of thoughts and impressions that sizzled for a second then seemed to disappear like water on a hot iron skillet were actually seeping His truth into my way of thinking. That was never more apparent than a recent review of personal journals in which I discovered ideas and phrasing I've used here with no recollection I'd written them years ago.

In the time between then and now, friends and family encouraged me to write. My response was always I had nothing to write about someone else hasn't covered. Plus, I have no name recognition, which I can tell you from my experience as a professional publisher, is usually an authorial death sentence.

Yet as I hope we've discovered, God can blow through a death sentence like a cannonball through *paper mache*. One day, as I journaled about Christ's prediction the Temple in Jerusalem would be destroyed, it struck me He was all about dismantling Judaism and replacing it with something greater (Luke 21:5-6). That's when God reached into my subconscious and resurrected the idea for this book—including the title. I realized what applied to the Temple applies to our bodies. Apparently, the incubation was over. It was time for Lazarus to come forth.

I checked a well-known online retailer, thinking surely someone had already written the same book with the same or similar title. Nope. Not there. Nada. Nyetsville. I couldn't believe it.

I put it off starting for a while, straddling the precarious line between hope and doubt, more convinced I was the victim of my own ill-fated wishful thinking than the Holy Spirit's leading. But I couldn't shake the feeling it was a book I would enjoy writing provided there was enough content to keep you, the reader, engaged and moving closer to our Savior.

Finally, He gently prompted me to show hesitation the door. I sat down at the kitchen table with a computer in one hand, my Bible in the other, and more prayers of dependence and pleas for guidance than I can count. It was me and Him, chiseling truth, one keystroke at a time. The rest, as they say, is history.

His history. His enablement. His power. His insight. His grace. In other words, I'm more keenly aware than you can imagine what you have on these pages is something far beyond my ability to produce. In a sheer act of undeserved kindness, the God of the parsec and Planck length (see chapter two) hyperextended the right hand of His grace and power, took hold of my heart and mind, and guided me along the furrows of His wisdom to reap and dispense His truth in a way, I pray, brings you clarity, inspiration, and hope.

I have relished the experience more than you know. The camaraderie He and I have enjoyed is, like Him, beyond words. The sheer joy of working with Him to produce it for you, the reader, has been worth every moment of effort. It has been, in the truest, deepest sense of the Word, a labor of Love—His for me, mine for Him, and ours for you. It has been an honor—and I pray You'll enjoy Him even more for having spent time here.

So as we close, I simply want to say, "Thanks." Thanks for believing the subject matter and the way He's directed me to express it have been worth your time. You are busy and have many choices when it comes to how you spend the precious days He gives us. I trust His work in me will encourage you that our status as massive jumbles of imperfection will one day be swallowed up in the great victory which is ours through faith in Him. He will send sin and death whimpering to the corner while we take our seat at the Great Banquet where... you guessed it... we'll discover there are no old people in heaven.

Until then, stay steady. Stay strong in Him. Stay at it. Each day you look in the mirror and spot one more wrinkle or age spot, another gray hair (or lack of one) just remind yourself *we live by faith, not by sight. What we see is the mirage. What He promises is real.* One day soon, friends, it will be ours. For the promise of its arrival—together with all the other promises He's given us—all praise to Him, our Sovereign God, King, Savior, and Friend.

> The heavens praise Your wonders, O LORD, Your faithfulness too, in the assembly of the holy ones. For who in the skies above can compare with the LORD? Who is like the LORD among the heavenly beings? In the council of the holy ones God is greatly feared; He is more awesome than all who surround him. O LORD God Almighty, who is like You? You are mighty, O LORD, and Your faithfulness surrounds You.
>
> PSALM 89:5 NIV

About the Author

Steve Lyon is a graduate of Dallas Theological Seminary and former youth pastor, staff writer for Gary Smalley and John Trent, senior pastor, and Christian publishing executive. He and his wife, Dawn, are—day by day—getting ready at their home in Cedar Park, Texas.

To contact Steve with questions or to book him for a speaking engagement, e-mail him at nopih595@gmail.com

Made in the USA
Monee, IL
09 April 2022

94410074R00096